Playscript 101

TWO PLAYS FOR THE RIGHT
The Loud Boy's Life
Birth on a Hard Shoulder

Howard Barker

JOHN CALDER · LONDON
RIVERRUN PRESS · NEW YORK

First published in Great Britain 1982 by
John Calder (Publishers) Ltd.,
18, Brewer Street,
London W1R 4AS

and in the USA 1982 by
Riverrun Press Inc.,
Suite 814, 175 Fifth Avenue,
New York, NY 10010

Copyright © Howard Barker, 1982

All performing rights in this play are strictly reserved and
applications for performances should be made to:
Judy Daish Associates Ltd.,
122 Wigmore Street,
London W1H 9FE

No performance of this play may be given unless a licence has been obtained
prior to rehearsal.

ALL RIGHTS RESERVED

British Library Cataloguing in Publication Data
Barker, Howard
    Two plays for the right.— (Playscript series; 101)
    I. Title
    822'.914   PR6052.A6485
    ISBN 0 7145 3896 5

ISBN 0 71453896 5 paperbound

Any paperback edition of this book whether published simultaneously
with, or subsequent to, the hardback edition is sold subject to the
condition that it shall not, by way of trade, be lent, resold, hired
out, or otherwise disposed of, without the publisher's consent, in
any form of binding or cover other than that in which it is published.

No part of this publication may be reproduced, stored in a retrieval
system, or transmitted in any form by any means, electronic,
mechanical, photocopying, recording or otherwise, except brief
extracts for the purpose of review, without the prior written
permission of the publisher and the copyright holder.

Typeset in 9/10 point Times by Gedset of Ged Lennox Design, Cheltenham.
Printed and bound in the Channel Islands by The Guernsey Press Company Ltd.

TWO PLAYS FOR THE RIGHT
The Loud Boy's Life
Birth on a Hard Shoulder

Middlesex University
WITHDRAWN
Library Services

No One Was Saved
Alpha Alpha
Edward, The Final Days
Stripwell
Claw
Fair Slaughter
The Love of a Good Man
That Good Between Us
The Hang of the Gaol
The Loud Boy's Life
No End of Blame

T.V. Plays

Cows
Mutinies
Prowling Offensive
Conrod
Heroes of Labour
Russia
All Bleeding
Heaven

Radio Plays

One Afternoon on the 63rd Level of the North Face
of the Pyramid of Cheops the Great
Henry V in Two Parts
Herman with Millie and Mick

CONTENTS

0714538965

Site TP	MIDDLESEX UNIVERSITY LIBRARY
Accession No.	9530565
Class No.	822.914 BAR
Special Collection ✓	

The Loud Boy's Life

A Note on the Text

The Loud Boy's Life was commissioned as a two-part television play by BBC TV. It was vehemently rejected on submission in 1980.

The play was conceived as a collage of biographical moments linked by a running theme—the making of a television series by Fricker himself on the subject of his favourite city, London. In the course of this enterprise Fricker and the film crew visited the crypt of St. Paul's, Clapham Junction, and the tomb of the Unknown Warrior, encountering the spirits of Lawrence of Arabia, Oscar Wilde and the Unknown Warrior himself.

The limitations of the Warehouse Theatre made so many changes of location impracticable, and for the stage version the making of the documentary was abandoned, some small parts of Fricker's commentary being retained as background during the frequent scene changes. These have been incorporated into the text. Fricker's funeral, which had been envisaged by me as a possible third episode for television, became an abbreviated final act.

Should the day arrive when television is liberated from its terror of the people and becomes an instrument of enlightenment rather than a modulator and manufacturer of public opinion, there may be an opportunity for this play to be seen in its entirety. Perhaps by then this examination of the ringing depths of the reactionary mind may have been rendered quaint by passing time. If, as I suspect, Fricker is always with us, then those curious to examine the original text will find it, like an unclaimed suicide, in a steel drawer at the BBC.

The Loud Boy's Life was first performed at the RSC's Warehouse Theatre, on 26 February 1980.

The cast were:

SHISH	Hugh Fraser
TOON	David John
BLINTER	Roger Sloman
EZRA FRICKER	Clive Merrison
CLENCH	Kenny Ireland
SKARDON	Fred Pearson
LEATHERS	Alun Armstrong
GREENO	Cheryl Hall
DEVOID	Donald Sumpter
COSTALL	Colin McCormack
MILMO	John Rogan
PULVERIST	Andrew Dickson
UPHOLSTERER	Kenny Ireland
FRONTAGE	Alun Armstrong
BACKLAWN	Hugh Fraser
DAMPSING	Colin McCormack
ANN ADUR	Matyelok Gibbs
SLYHOOP	Fred Pearson
CRYSTAL BACKLAWN	Jill Baker
GERMAN BOMBER	Andrew Dickson
SOLDIER 1	Roger Sloman
SOLDIER 2	David John
CAMBERLEY	Roger Sloman
PINCER	Kenny Ireland
BAKER	Alun Armstrong
SATCHLEY	Matyelok Gibbs
SERVANT	John Rogan
DOGGITT	Fred Pearson
DORIS FRICKER	Cheryl Hall
TUESDAY	Andrew Dickson
IMBER	Colin McCormack
WIPER	Hugh Fraser
SLAPP	David John
DR MALLOW	Donald Sumpter
SIR GEORGE FLEMING	John Rogan
STALLHOLDER	Kenny Ireland
NATLEY	David John
ALAN STREATHAM	Colin McCormack
TICE	John Rogan
SLADE	Clive Merrison
EADY	Roger Sloman
JEAL	Hugh Fraser
NOYES	Andrew Dickson

Directed by Howard Davies.
Designed by Douglas Heap.

ACT ONE

Scene One

To No. 38 Air 'Why Do The Nations?' from Handel's Messiah. A baroque banqueting hall somewhere in the City of London, with three WAITERS *laying the finishing touches to long, prepared tables.*

The WAITERS *stand with napkins over their arms, in assigned places. Long pause.*

SHISH.   I wish I was a girl. *(Pause.)* I would have such brief knickers on. *(Pause.)* More like a pencil-line. Of silver ciré. Glinting in the shadow of my crack. *(Pause.)* And my titties would be—*(Pause.)* Rising and falling. *(Pause.)* Rising and falling. *(Pause.)* How could he resist me? He would be lifting the mahogany.

TOON.   Not Ezra. Ezra would not stir for that.

SHISH.   I'd tilt my hips. Contrive to bring my bum cheeks near his wiry nostrils.

TOON.   Not our Ezra.

SHISH.   Work on him, I would. Coax him with the toing and froing of my female skin.

TOON.   Roy, Ezra is a public figure.

SHISH.   Figures have got feelings.

BLINTER.   This is rather academic, Roy.

SHISH.   Given I am trapped in my own gender.

BLINTER.   Given the Ancient Order of Savages will have no skirt. *(Murmuring in the corridor beyond.)*

TOON.   I hear our lords and masters of the night.

BLINTER.   I hate this lot. I hate all ancient orders.

TOON.   They drop pound notes like dung at a gymkhana, Mick . . . .

BLINTER.   I hate them all the more for it.

TOON.   Mick is a true professional. Full of contempt for the excessive gratuity. Mick is a massive loather, aren't you, Mick? *(There is a high-pitched laugh outside.)*

SHISH.   Ezra's laugh. I heard it at the Mansion House.

TOON.   A high laugh. In the eunuch register.

SHISH.   The whinny of a genius.

BLINTER.   This is the last year I serve the Savages. I'm only here because Ezra is the honoured guest.

SHISH.   I wish I had suspenders on . . . Black belt, no lace. And stocking welts four inches deep . . . *(The murmurs are loud.)*

TOON.   On your marks.

BLINTER.   I won't be maimed. Tonight I chuck the crystal back.

SHISH.   Oh, Ezra Fricker, how I love your vocal tones, you prince among these stale and groiny geezers!

The Ancient Order of Savages appears in the double doors. The leading figure, CLENCH, *beats the floor with a ceremonial pole. There is instant silence.*

CLENCH.   Gentlemen, the feeling for the breasts! *(The Order comes singly into the room. As each man steps in, his dinner jacket undone in readiness,* CLENCH *lays his right hand formally on the breast.)* Pass into our company. *(The man goes to his place at the table.)* Pass into our company. *(The next follows suit.)* Pass into our company. *(And so on.)* Pass into our company. *(The ceremony continues in silence until the last of the Order has been ritually examined. Then* CLENCH *beats the floor again.)* I confirm I have examined for woman according to the statutes of the order. *(Pause.)* Seal the doors. *(*TOON *locks the doors, hands the key to* CLENCH. *At once everybody sits and begins talking.)* Who 'ad my fags? *(A packet is tossed to him as he makes his way to the top table.)* Thank you, Raymond. *(He looks in the packet.)* Always the gentleman, 'e 'as left me one. Mr. Fricker, the last of my treasure?

FRICKER *(Seated next to him at the top table).*   Thank you, I have my own somewhat eccentric cigarettes.

CLENCH.   House of Commons King Size?

FRICKER.   A private blend.

CLENCH.   A private blend? Of what, may I enquire?

FRICKER.   Well, certainly you may enquire. I feel sure you'll understand if I decline to tell you. It is, after all, the definition of private, that the thing in question is not shared. *(He smiles.)*

CLENCH.   Indeed. *(Pause.)* Yes. *(He smiles.)* Very good. *(*FRICKER *lights one of his own.* CLENCH *rises to his feet, strikes the table with a gavel.)* Gentlemen, gentlemen, the toast is the Ancient Order of Savages, and the Right Honourable Ezra Fricker, MP. *(The Order stands, raise their glasses.)*

ALL.   **The Ancient Order of Savages and the Right Honourable Ezra Fricker, MP.**

They all sit. FRICKER *rises to reply to the toast. He waits for a perfect silence.*

FRICKER.   This is an honour now rare within the jurisdiction of the British parliament. It is, unwillingly, a somewhat secret practice where the royal writ runs. For parliament has in its wisdom deemed us an assembly, if not immoral, if not unlawful, then far worse, anachronistic. And God help you if you are anachronistic—*(Cries of 'Hear! Hear!)* You have no chance. Better you are out of work than out of date, the courts will have no mercy on you! *(Laughter and applause.)* We hear a great deal about liberty. I am inclined to invoke the thing myself. Liberty is on everybody's lips. It is a liberty-taking society. And yet I must tell you, liberty is a commodity like any other, it is a commodity not unlike biscuits. The more you take, the less stay in the packet. A lot demand their absolute and inalienable right to biscuits. And the result is that the fund of liberty, like the biscuit barrel, is not greater, but is less! *(Applause and 'Hear! Hear!'* FRICKER *waits for it to subside.)* Discrimination

(Pause.) Now, there is a word. *(Pause.)* What a word it is. All five syllables of it. *(Pause.)* A word which has suffered, as words can—they are not unlike us in this respect—a terrible change of fortune. One day they are worthy words, and the next—*(He shakes his head glumly.)* It is amazing what can happen in the stock market of vocabulary. *(Laughter and table thumping.)* Once upon a time—I can remember it—if you were discriminating you were fastidious and a man of taste. You preferred The Times to The Sun. You knew steak tartare from chicken in the basket. *(Laughter.)* Now, if you are discriminating you are guilty of an offence. *(Pause. He shrugs.)* Well, it's a word's life. *(Ripple of laughter.)* Gentlemen, this word, the pejorative of all pejoratives, is now canonized within the body of the English law. With all my powers of debate, with all that which my friends are pleased to call my eloquence, I could not block its coronation.

SOME. Shame, shame . . . *(Pause.)*

FRICKER. Tonight, therefore, I find myself in a situation of the utmost delicacy. On the one hand I am a member of that august body, the legislature of the land, and on the other, the honoured guest of outlaws. *(Laughter.)* Under the circumstances, I shall satisfy myself by a simple observation. *(He peers ostentatiously round the room, hand above his eyes.)* Odd. There are no ladies present.

Roars of laughter and applause as FRICKER *takes his seat. He recovers his cigarette from the ashtray. The* WAITERS *go round the tables.*

SKARDON. Norman, this is Miles. Miles, Norman. Norman is chief constable. Miles is Charlie Greeno's son. Charlie could not come.

LEATHERS. There has not been an Englishman like this since Winston.

SKARDON. I thought Winston. Winston comes to mind.

LEATHERS. Who tempers discipline with wit. I find no end of discipline is possible with wit.

SKARDON. Norman is the last strong copper.

LEATHERS. Ralph is the last soft magistrate.

SKARDON. Norman has been spared the university.

LEATHERS. I have no doctorates. I wear boots.

SKARDON. He rose by stages from the beat. From dog-handler, Norman, wasn't it?

LEATHERS. I won a shield with Sheba.

SKARDON. Never knew her.

LEATHERS. Bitch Dobermann. On my mantelpiece.

SKARDON. The dog?

LEATHERS. The shield, daft arse. *(He looks to* GREENO, *sitting between them.)* Do you love dogs?

GREENO. I hate dogs.

LEATHERS. No one can hate a dog.

GREENO. I do.

LEATHERS. Not hate, son.

GREENO. Yes.

LEATHERS. Bitten as a baby, were you? Nipped in the pram?

GREENO. No.

LEATHERS.   Must have been, and you've forgotten it.

SKARDON.   Norman, Miles does not like dogs.

GREENO.   They bite to order and shit at will.

LEATHERS.   What's wrong with shit?

GREENO.   Wrong with shit?

LEATHERS.   I shit. You shit. Do you shit, Ralph?

SKARDON.   Not as frequently as I would like.

LEATHERS.   But you do shit?

GREENO.   It's not the function I object to.

LEATHERS.   Glad to hear it.

GREENO.   It's the distribution.

LEATHERS *(calling)*.   Mr Fricker, what's your policy on dog-shit? *(Laughter.)*

FRICKER.   I am of the opinion that the sole distinction to be made between a good law and a bad law is that the former is enforceable. I would suggest that there are three areas in which the law has got no business — micturition, defaecation, and fornication. *(Roars of laughter and applause.)*

LEATHERS.   No risk of the latter here tonight.

FRICKER.   I trust not.

DEVOID.   Risk? He calls it risk!

FRICKER.   Risk, yes! It is an activity replete with risk!

COSTALL.   Infection, Mr Fricker?

MILMO.   The female organ is the perfect culture bed for bacillus.

FRICKER.   Is that so?

MILMO.   Warm, wet, and flushed with dying matter at four week intervals. A pocket to be dipped in at your peril. I speak as a surgeon. I speak as a female specialist.

FRICKER.   I was not thinking of infection, at least not in a medical sense. I was thinking of the moral destruction consequent upon excessive indulgence in the act.

DEVOID.   Fucking—tarts—fucks—you. *(He grins.)*

FRICKER.   The gentleman is not one for fancy metaphors.

DEVOID.   Fucking—tarts—fucks—you.

CLENCH.   Mr Devoid is a novelist.

DEVOID.   I fucking am.

FRICKER.   The sentiment, I dare say, is by and large correct.

DEVOID.   I love the darlings.

FRICKER.   Well, who am I to quarrel with the interpretation of a word like love? It carries about as much meaning as a string bag carries water.

DEVOID.   I do not mean I love them.

FRICKER.   Ah.

DEVOID.   You are so pedantic you give me shooting pains right through my arse.

CLENCH.   Andrew . . .

SKARDON.   Come on, Andrew.

DEVOID.   I apologize *(Pause.)* I do not mean I love them. When I say I love them I mean I want to poke them. **All of them**.

MILMO.   Andrew is pissed.

CLENCH. Andrew, this is the annual dinner of the Savages.

DEVOID. Yes. And I have eaten it.

BLINTER. This is how it all began last year. This is the overture to six stitches in my head.

MILMO. Andy, do your woman.

DEVOID. No.

CLENCH. I think we would prefer to—

MILMO. Do your fucked housewife, come on —

DEVOID. No!

CLENCH. Monty, do we—

DEVOID. Not ready yet.

PULVERIST *(rising, striking the table three times with his fist).* I call upon— *(The assembly takes it up.)* I call upon — *(He looks round the faces.)* I call upon—fellow Savage—*(He looks, as they thump.)* Leathers!

LEATHERS. Oh, blimey.

PULVERIST. To entertain us with his **wife**.

LEATHERS. Oh, bloody 'ell.

SKARDON. Good luck, Norman.

LEATHERS. Why is it always me?

MILMO. Come on Norman!

COSTALL. Get on with it!

Reluctantly, LEATHERS *stands up. He ponders for a moment, then screwing up his face into a mask of parody, screeches falsetto.*

LEATHERS. Not gonna swallow it! Don't wanna swallow it! Don't 'ave to swallow it!

He imitates a choking sensation. Laughter and clapping.

FRICKER'S LONDON. ON THE SURREY DOCKS.

Fricker's Voice

Let it not be said that in my love for this great city I take you only to the hackneyed spots. I am not some Leica or Yashica-popping tourist bundled from his air-conditioned bedroom into the hygienic splendours of the all-seeing but never-knowing panoramic bus. No, I stand now not on mown turf, but on a field of rubble, because it is rubble London carries in her heart, it is a rubble city, shedding its buildings, whether from war or profit, like so many skins. Let a building feel never so proud, resounding as it may do to the heeltaps of elegant and perfumed secretaries, its fate is rubble, rubble awaits it at its end. What rubble is this, then, this dusty yellow brick crumbling in my fingers, a London brick, a stock brick of the nineteenth century, a little green as if it once knew water? I am standing, believe it or not, in the middle of the Surrey docks. And is the silence not most eloquent? There are no vessels hooting here. I could be in the middle of the Gobi Desert. I doubt London has ever known such vast and eerie silences since Hadrian quartered the XIV Legion here. Such is the mockery of History, the turning of the tables on what was once the goods-collecting, goods-producing and goods-delivering cockpit of the world. Alas, trade is abolished here, and the activity, like the word, despatched into the knacker's yard.

Scene Two

An evening in Greenwich Park, 1942. A blitz is in progress. A group of people approach in coats and hats carrying hampers. They are lit by gunflashes.

UPHOLSTERER.   Anybody bringing chairs? Lionel? Anybody bringing chairs?

FRONTAGE.   Got a lilo.

UPHOLSTERER.   Got a lilo. Marvellous.

FRONTAGE.   Bernard, please don't grumble. Don't start off the evening grumbling, please.

BACKLAWN.   A German plane is low-pitched. In the key of G.

DAMPSING.   The Heinkel.

BACKLAWN.   The Heinkel, yes, is G. Except when diving.

DAMPSING.   I think she knows that, don't you, Ann? That diving changes the pitch?

ADUR.   I think I do.

BACKLAWN.   There is the Heinkel. There is the G.

FRONTAGE.   We are rather near the anti-aircraft battery.

SLYHOOP.   I think eveyone gathered that.

FRONTAGE *(on his knees blowing up a lilo)*.   Anybody else fancy a blow?

SLYHOOP.   All the high ground has been grabbed by the artillery. If you want a decent view of London you have to put up with the artillery.

FRONTAGE *(to FRICKER who is gazing over the blazing city)*.   Ezra, would you be so good as to help out with a blow?

BACKLAWN.   Now, that's a Hurricane. That whine. Night-fighting Hurricane.

DAMPSING.   High C.

FRONTAGE.   Ezra?

BACKLAWN.   A Stuka would be higher still. Would be unmistakable.

UPHOLSTERER.   I want to sit now.

FRONTAGE.   Yes, I know.

DAMPSING.   I haven't heard a Stuka.

BACKLAWN.   Really?

ADUR.   Shall I get the glasses out?

CRYSTAL *(rivetted by the burning docks)*.   The docks are burning. The actual concrete is alight.

FRICKER.   Yes . . .

CRYSTAL.   And all these little bits of paper, like blazing butterflies out of Millwall . . .

FRICKER.   Yes . . . Yes . . .

BACKLAWN.   A ship! They got a ship!

FRONTAGE.   Everybody wants to watch and no one wants to get the supper out.

UPHOLSTERER.   I must sit, Lionel.

FRONTAGE.   I know, I know.

ADUR.   I can't open bottles. Someone, please?

UPHOLSTERER.   I'm sitting.

BACKLAWN.   Heinkel in the searchlights!

SLYHOOP/DAMPSING.   Where? Where?

DAMPSING.   Four o'clock.

ADUR/SLYHOOP.   Where? Where?

BAKLAWN.   Lost it.

FRONTAGE *(as* UPHOLSTERER *plumps down).*   Thank you, Bernard!

ADUR.   What's the matter?

FRONTAGE.   Bernard must sit on the lilo. All the fucking air's gone out of it.

ADUR.   Somebody help Lionel.

FRONTAGE.   I cannot inflate the lilo while somebody is sitting on it.

UPHOLSTERER.   I am not getting up.

FRONTAGE.   Then we have no lilo, do we?

FRICKER.   This is the most extraordinary spectacle. They are setting light to London, London is burning, and the air is charged with futile chattering . . .

CRYSTAL.   I hate them.

FRICKER.   Oh, no.

CRYSTAL.   Yes, I hate them.

FRICKER.   I don't think you should hate them. It is the essence of history.

BACKLAWN.   The gunners are arcing now. They are arcing, Ann, to keep the raiders up.

DAMPSING.   They are not arcing. They are firing in a grid.

BACKLAWN.   They are arcing, Gavin.

DAMPSING.   No, it's a grid.

BACKLAWN.   Got a balloon! A balloon's been hit!

CRYSTAL.   My husband is an idiot.

FRICKER.   Yes, I'm afraid I think he is.

CRYSTAL.   And not lovable. Simply an idiot.

FRICKER *(gazing into the docklands).*   There are people down there . . .

CRYSTAL.   Crouching in the underground. Clasping their cats . . . *(Pause.)* I would like it if you made love to me. *(Pause.)*

FRICKER.   I am deeply honoured.

CRYSTAL.   Yes, but do you want to?

FRICKER.   I must say I am taken with your sense of history.

CRYSTAL.   Yes. But do you want to have a fuck? *(Pause.)*

FRICKER.   Yes. *(Pause.)* Please.

CRYSTAL.   Good. *(A champagne cork pops.)*

ADUR.   Bernard wants to propose a toast!

SLYHOOP.   Gather round Bernard, everyone!

DAMPSING.   Bernard's toast!

They gather round UPHOLSTERER, *who is on the ground, take glasses and wait.*

UPHOLSTERER *(raising his own glass).*   The death of England.

CRYSTAL.   No. Sorry, Bernard. Absolutely no no no.

UPHOLSTERER.   Who paid for the liquor?

FRONTAGE.   I really don't see that entitles anyone —

UPHOLSTERER.   Who paid for the liquor?

FRICKER.   Bernard, I know this is your party, but I do think you should show a little more gratitude to your friends in the Home Office that they have not consigned you to some draughty internment camp. Could you not be satisfied with something like the King's health?

UPHOLSTERER.   No!

ADUR.   Bernard, you like the king!

UPHOLSTERER.   No!

BACKLAWN.   I will propose a toast.

UPHOLSTERER.   The death of England.

FRONTAGE.   We are not having that as a toast.

CRYSTAL.   Bernard, if you say that again, I will chuck my glass straight at your gob.

BACKLAWN.   The working people. *(He raises his glass.)*

CRYSTAL.   No. That is disgusting. That is obscene. They are being burned alive down there.

BACKLAWN.   Meant well.

CRYSTAL.   Of course you did. But it remains obscene.

DAMPSING.   Shall we perhaps dispense with toasts?

CRYSTAL.   I have a toast.

FRONTAGE.   Good.

CRYSTAL.   To feeling.

ADUR.   Feeling?

CRYSTAL.   Feeling. Yes. I like feeling.

FRICKER.   Feeling. *(They all drink.)* I have an horror. That they will bring the House of Commons down.

SLYHOOP.   Ezra wants to be prime minister.

FRICKER.   There is no worthier ambition.

ADUR.   I have a brother in Cyrenaica. All the soldiers hate the politicians there. More than the Germans.

FRICKER.   It has always been difficult to persuade soldiers of the wisdom of civilian government. Something happens to a citizen when he dons uniform. He dons arrogance along with badges it appears.

CRYSTAL.   Do you want to fuck or not?

SLYHOOP.   The sausage rolls are dying of neglect.

DAMPSING.   Drink, anyone. Darling, can I top you up?

CRYSTAL.   No.

DAMPSING *(moving on.)* Bernard?

CRYSTAL.   Casually wander over there.

FRONTAGE *(from the hamper.)* Christ! There's a bloody great iron thing in the flan!

BACKLAWN.   Shrapnel.

FRONTAGE.   My bloody flan . . .

BACKLAWN.   Falling all around us. Hear it? Sharpnel.

UPHOLSTERER.   Terrible error, burning the docks. We got some of our best lads from the docks. Some muscle! Some knuckle! They will never wear their black shirts now. Not now their grannies have had Krupp of Essen on their heads . . .

FRICKER.   War is the Rude Man of History. He does not say excuse me as he shoulders your ambitions off the kerb.

UPHOLSTERER.   Who said that?

FRICKER.   I did.

UPHOLSTERER.   Liar. You are only 23.

FRICKER.   A free translation of the Greek. Fricker out of Herodotus.

UPHOLSTERER.   What do you know about history?

FRICKER.   I have just left Oxford with a triple first.

UPHOLSTERER.   My right arm's lying in the Somme.

FRICKER.   Yes. Well, I should not like to choose between our qualifications.

UPHOLSTERER.   When I was your age all I wanted to do was fuck.

FRICKER.   Fair enough.

UPHOLSTERER.   There is a woman there wants you to stuff her.

FRICKER.   Yes.

UPHOLSTERER.   What's the matter with you?

FRICKER.   Me?

UPHOLSTERE.   Get on with it.

FRICKER.   No rush.

UPHOLSTERER.   **No rush? No rush?**

FRICKER.   Bernard, you are drowning the ack-acks . . .

UPHOLSTERER.   **No fucking rush?**

FRICKER.   That's what I said. *(He turns to the view.)* Look, they're switching their attack to the Surrey Commercial.

SLYHOOP.   London will cease to exist . . .

DAMPSING.   The River Thames has been the trouble in this war. It leads straight into London. Any boss-eyed Italian pilot only has to follow it.

ADUR.   Mussolini's son-in-law has dropped incendiaries in Southwark.

SLYHOOP.   Only Ann would know a thing like that.

ADUR.   It was headlines in Corriere del Sierra. Four days running. Only they could not spell Southwark.

DAMPSING.   Ann thinks we've lost the war, don't you Ann?

ADUR.   It's the view of the civil service.

SLYHOOP.   I have six thousand shares in Fahben, Düsseldorf. What I should be aiming for is a long war ending in a German victory. Is that very likely, Ann?

ADUR.   We are forecasting a Russian capitulation in six weeks.

SLYHOOP.   Ah . . .

ADUR.   England to negotiate in 1943.

BACKLAWN.   I wish someone would get me in a ministry.

ADUR.   The King will go to Canada. Hitler will ride the length of Oxford Street in the Coronation Coach. Only officers will be billeted in postal districts beginning with a W.

FRICKER.   Ann is a mine of information.

ADUR.   I am a good civil servant.

FRICKER.   Though not excessively discreet. I ask myself what Ann will do in the event of the prophesied, nay, inevitable Nazi victory?

ADUR.   Remain at my post, naturally.

FRICKER.   Naturally, she says. It has the ring of heroism, does it not? Like the gunner boy at Jutland. Any order that comes down the telephone she will obey, even if the accent is a trifle gutteral.

SLYHOOP.   Well, naturally! What will you do, Fricker?

FRICKER.   I am at the King's disposal, aren't I? It is his uniform I wear.

UPHOLSTERER.   Which king?

FRICKER *(with feigned naïvete)*. Which king? Is there more than one?

UPHOLSTERER.   The king across the water. *(Pause.)*.

FRICKER.   The king who has been crowned according to the custom of the English people.

DAMPSING.   Ezra is a sly one.

FRICKER.   Sly? How am I sly?

DAMPSING.   Because they'll crown him, won't they? This time.

FRICKER *(pointing.)* Look! A halo of fire around St. Paul's! All the magic of great Englishmen, straining in their vaults, has kept the bombs away from it!

SLYHOOP.   No, it's the domed roof. The incendiaries slide off it.

CRYSTAL *(beside* FRICKER*)*. Where the fuck have you been?

FRICKER.   I —

CRYSTAL.   I have wandered away three times now.

FRICKER.   Got into an argument with Bernard.

CRYSTAL.   Listen, do you like me?

FRICKER.   Yes.

CRYSTAL.   No. You know what I mean. Like me?

FRICKER.   Yes.

CRYSTAL.   Think I'm tasty?

FRICKER.   Exactly.

CRYSTAL.   You could really eat me, couldn't you?

FRICKER.   Quite. *(Pause. She looks at him.)*

CRYSTAL.   Good. No point in bothering otherwise. *(Pause.)* I will be under the rowan tree. *(She looks at him with slight suspicion, then moves off.)*

DAMPSING *(watching her drift away)*.   Crystal doesn't like us.

BACKLAWN.   She has to be alone at times.

DAMPSING.   Not all the time.

BACKLAWN.   I don't know much about Crystal, Dampsing, so don't ask me.

DAMPSING.   Isn't she your wife?

BACKLAWN.   Don't be clever. There's a good chap.

FRONTAGE *(pointing skywards)*.   **Got one! They got one!**

SLYHOOP.   Burning! It's bloody burning!

FRONTAGE.   Got one! Got one!

SLYHOOP.   Bits are dropping off of it . . .

BACKLAWN.   Messerschmidt 109E.

DAMPSING.   Got two engines . . .

BACKLAWN.   I said don't be clever, didn't I?

DAMPSING.   Ann?

ADUR.   It's a Junkers 88.

FRONTAGE.   It's coming over here . . .

SLYHOOP.   So it is.

FRONTAGE.   **Christ! It's coming over here!**

UPHOLSTERER *(waving a glass)*.   **Hooray! Come on, you bastard! Scrape our guts over the ground!**

Everyone scatters, but for UPHOLSTERER *who rocks with laughter, falling off backwards from the lilo. Sound of a heavy plane passing low. Pause.*

Some moments afterwards, a parachute floats out of the sky. The BOMBER *rolls into a heap, picks himself up, releases his harness. He looks round, sees the hamper.*

BOMBER.   Hallo? Bitte? Hallo? *(He goes to the hamper, takes up a champagne bottle, puts it to his lips.)*

UPHOLSTERER *(sitting up).*   A vengeance shall come out of the East . . .

BOMBER *(turning, raising his hands).*   Surrender under the terms of the Geneva Convention! *(Pause.* UPHOLSTERER *grins.)*

UPHOLSTERER.   Gott strafe England! *(Pause.)*

BOMBER.   Bitte?

UPHOLSTERER.   Come on, you silly bastard! The New Order! Heil! *(Pause.)*

BOMBER.   Surrender under the terms of the Geneva Convention!

UPHOLSTERER *(shaking his head).*   Oh my God . . .

BOMBER.   Bitte?

UPHOLSTERER.   The Master Race . . . *(He points some distance away.)* Over there. Under the Rowan tree. *(*BOMBER *looks puzzled.)* Unter den Linden. Go on, son!

BOMBER.   Surrender under the —

UPHOLSTERER.   **Fraulein, yer stupid sod!**

BOMBER *shrugs, walks uncertainly away, taking the bottle.*

Scene Three

Another part of Greenwich Park. CRYSTAL *and the* BOMBER *are seated side by side, overlooking London.*

CRYSTAL.   Down there . . . Down there . . . are hundreds of thousands . . . of people . . . actual people . . .

BOMBER.   Ja.

CRYSTAL.   No, don't touch my knee. I am telling you something.

BOMBER.   Ja.

CRYSTAL.   Being killed. Being blown to smithereens. Do you know what smithereens are?

BOMBER.   Ja.

CRYSTAL.   I know I have nice knees. I do not want you to handle them.

BOMBER.   Bitte?

CRYSTAL.   Some are children. Some are tiny babies. And you have been murdering them. You are a murderer.

BOMBER.   Ja.

CRYSTAL.   **A mur-der-er.**

BOMBER.   Ja.

CRYSTAL.   Because you have a funny outfit on does not mean you are not a murderer. You have just been murdering my people.

BOMBER.   Geneva!
CRYSTAL.   I know all about Geneva.
BOMBER.   Geneva . . .
CRYSTAL.   I think they should hang you. Geneva or not. That would stop it.
   In fact I think Geneva is a very good place to hang people like you
BOMBER *(putting his hand on her thigh)*.   England — is — good ja?
CRYSTAL.   Look, I am not going to fuck with you. You are an enemy. My
   city is burning. I love my city. **Look at it!** *(She removes his hand force-
   fully. He takes a swig at the champagne. hands it to her. She drinks
   some.)* I draw the line at fascists. I will fuck with all sorts, but no fascist
   gets his thing near me. (BOMBER *takes out a fistful of Reichsmarks and
   holds them out.)* No. Absolutely bloody no. (BOMBER *looks pleadingly
   at her. Then makes a grab for her. She screams.* FRICKER *rushes up
   waving his service revolver. He points it, shaking, and shoots.)*

FRICKER.   **I have killed a German! I have killed a German!**
CRYSTAL.   Will you get him off me?
FRICKER.   **Oh, God, I have slain the enemy!**
CRYSTAL.   Just get him off me!
FRICKER.   **I have delivered us! Oh, Lord, I have delivered us!**
BOMBER.   Mutte! Mutte!
CRYSTAL.   He is bleeding all over me!
BOMBER.   Mutte! Mutte!
CRYSTAL.   I am not your mutte! Ugh! Look at his arm!
FRICKER.   **Field dressing!**
CRYSTAL.   Will you put that gun away!
FRICKER *(waving it)*.   **You are my prisoner!**
CRYSTAL *(to* FRICKER*)*.   Try to relax. Please. Relax.
FRICKER *(dancing with the gun)*.   I can't. I can't.
CRYSTAL.   Sit down and take deep breaths. *(The* BOMBER *groans.)* All
   three of us. Deep breaths.
FRICKER *(sitting)*.   I have never shot a man before.
CRYSTAL.   All right.
FRICKER.   **Look at my hands!**
CRYSTAL.   Shh!
FRICKER.   **My hands!**
CRYSTAL.   Give me your hands. *(She takes them, draws a deep breath.)* In.
   (BOMBER *and* FRICKER *breathe in.)* Out. *(They all exhale.)*
FRICKER/CRYSTAL.   In. *(Pause.)* Out. *(They breathe a few times.)*
FRICKER.   My father is a lay preacher. He exorteth me to smite mine enemy.
CRYSTAL.   You are not breathing.
FRICKER.   He commandeth me to scatter the transgressor.
CRYSTAL.   In.
FRICKER.   What can I do?
CRYSTAL.   Out. *(They breathe a few more times.)*
FRICKER.   If I told you I felt chosen, would you laugh at me?
CRYSTAL.   Chosen for what?
FRICKER.   To lead my race. *(Pause.)*
CRYSTAL.   I think you should volunteer for active service at the earliest
   opportunity.

FRICKER. Yes.

CRYSTAL. The commandos, preferably.

FRICKER. Yes. All right. Now make love to me.

CRYSTAL. No.

FRICKER. Why not?

CRYSTAL. You've just shot somebody.

FRICKER. Yes, and I feel full of confidence.

CRYSTAL. That's what worries me.

FRICKER. **I order you!**

CRYSTAL. You see?

FRICKER. No, all right, I don't order you. Of course I don't order you, I earnestly request you.

CRYSTAL *(getting up).* I am going home for a bath. I am rather bloody.

FRICKER. Listen — I have not had much to do with beautiful women, Mrs. Backlawn. To be completely frank. But I have studied them. I have gone along pavements and breathed the air their movement stirred.

CRYSTAL. Peculiar.

FRICKER. No. Not peculiar. A little unconventional, perhaps. But very economical from the point of view of time. I wonder if you'd marry me?

CRYSTAL. I'm already married.

FRICKER. Oh, yes. So you are. But listen —

CRYSTAL. Ask again after the war. Look us up. We're in the book.

FRICKER. Thank you. I will.

CRYSTAL. Good.

FRICKER. You see, I shan't be killed.

CRYSTAL. I hope not.

FRICKER. I shan't be.

CRYSTAL. Some people are.

FRICKER. Even in the commandos. Even on a very, very foolish raid. Even on the most misconceived and futile mission, I will come through. *(Pause. She looks at him.)*

CRYSTAL. I think that is just the sort of attitude our commandos need.

FRICKER. You are determined not to take me seriously. I frighten you.

CRYSTAL. No.

FRICKER. The historical individual sets up eddies all around him in which others drown or swim. He exercises fascination.

CRYSTAL. We all know about fascination. What about the truth?

FRICKER. Truth?

CRYSTAL. Yes. You know. Truth.

FRICKER. History is truth.

CRYSTAL. Ah.

FRICKER. There is the truth. London, in her ashes, is the truth. *(Pause.)*

CRYSTAL. Well, I think I had better find my husband.

FRICKER. I suppose you had. *(She starts to go, stops.)*

CRYSTAL. I proposed a toast to feeling. I wonder if you have any.

FRICKER. I have a feeling I will save the English race.

CRYSTAL. That isn't really what I meant . . . *(She goes away.* FRICKER *looks at* BOMBER.*)*

FRICKER.   That is a feeling surely? If that is not a feeling I don't know what is.
    What are your feelings?
BOMBER.   Surrender under the terms of the Geneva Convention!
FRICKER.   Fear. Fear is your feeling. *(Some* SOLDIERS *rush in, waving
    rifles.)*
SOLDIER 1.   Woman says a German!
SOLDIER 2.   Got a German?
SOLDIER 1.   Here's the bugger!
SOLDIER 2.   Up you bugger!
SOLDIER 1.   Cover me! *(They wave their rifles menacingly.)*
SOLDIER 2.   Poke the bugger!
SOLDIER 1.   German! German!*(They prance round the bewildered*
    BOMBER.*)*
SOLDIER 2.   Poke 'im! Look at 'im! German! German! *(Makes a feint at the*
    BOMBER.*)* Cover me!
FRICKER.   I wonder if you gentlemen would care to issue me a chit?
SOLDIER 1.   A chit?
FRICKER.   For my prisoner.
SOLDIER 2.   A chit.
SOLDIER 1.   Give the gentleman officer a chit.
FRICKER.   Saying you took possession.
SOLDIER 1.   You got a chit?
FRICKER.   I take it we have not brought vast numbers of the enemy to the
    ground? *(Suddenly the soldier stops, letting his rifle droop.)*
SOLDIER 2.   'E's crying . . .
SOLDIER 1.   Oi. Fritz.
SOLDIER 2.   Crying . . .
SOLDIER 1.   Fritz?

*In silence they all watch him weep, their rifles hanging in their hands. A voice
calls out of the darkness.*

UPHOLSTERER.   Why doncha kiss him better? **Get along!** *(The*
    SOLDIERS *move off with the* BOMBER *dragging their guns and slovenly.*
    UPHOLSTERER *and* FRICKER *watch them go.)* In '16 took a pillbox
    with a pistol and a dagger with forty occupants inside. We were a different
    people then. We bled freely. We knew how to bleed. Even if we weren't sure
    why.
FRICKER.   Extraordinary spectacle. At first I thought they were out to
    murder him . . .
UPHOLSTERER.   More scared than he was.
FRICKER.   Yes! Yes, they were!
UPHOLSTERER.   War is all fear. When fear goes, fraternization rears its
    head. Stoke them with it, or they will roll in one another's arms.
BACKLAWN *(appearing).*   Anybody seen my Mrs? *(He looks at* FRICKER
    who is lost in thought.) Ezra? Seen my Mrs!
FRICKER.   I don't think so . . . no . . .
FRONTAGE.   Raid's nearly over, Bernard.
BACKLAWN.   Seen Crystal, anyone?
FRONTAGE.   All clear's sounding.

FRICKER.   Fear, you see . . .

BACKLAWN.   What?

FRICKER.   **Fear! Bind them with fear!**

BACKLAWN.   No, I'm looking for Crystal . . . *(He drifts away. Sound of the all clear.)*

FRONTAGE.   Anybody not handed their glasses in?

DAMPSING *(gazing over London).*   St. Paul's is still standing.

SLYHOOP.   Somerset House . . .

FRICKER *(wandering).*   I have the terms of my mission! I have the key which will unlock the stagnant passions of the English race!

ADUR.   Do you know you talk to yourself?

FRICKER *(stops, pauses).*   We all open our hearts to the one we love the best.

ADUR.   How sad. When you are only twenty-three.

FRICKER.   I don't think I was ever young. I am hoping, by the same token, I shall never be old either.

ADUR.   Futile.

FRICKER.   Is it?

ADUR.   You have no fun and you get old just the same as anybody else.

FRICKER.   I see. Well, you have all the answers. *(She turns to go; stops.)*

ADUR.   By the way, Crystal disappeared with Frank. *(Pause.)*

FRICKER.   Why are you telling me?

ADUR.   No reason.

FRICKER.   All right. She disappeared with Frank. *(Pause.)* Who is Frank, anyway? *(She shrugs.)*

ADUR.   Sorry.

FRICKER.   It's Backlawn you should be talking to, not me.

ADUR.   Sorry.

FRICKER.   He is her husband, isn't he?

ADUR.   Quite. Only I thought —

FRICKER.   You thought? **You thought?** No, no. Not to be recommended, in your case. Best not undertaken. Leave thought to those best qualified to manage it. *(She walks away. He wanders a little, runs his hand through his hair.)* This is a nuisance. This is an impediment. This feeling I have that I want — that she —

DAMPSING.   Ezra!

FRICKER.   Means something.

DAMPSING.   We're going down to Roger's club.

FRICKER.   Thank you.

DAMPSING.   Coming?

FRICKER.   No. I think I may—wander the streets. *(DAMPSING shrugs, disappears. FRICKER sits on the grass, stares over the city. Pause.)* Haec femina—mihi—inquieta—est . . .   *(Pause.)* Haec—Crystal—non—bona —fide—est . . . *(Pause.)* To Mrs Backlawn. In the style of Ovid, September, 1942.

FRICKER'S LONDON. ON THE TOWER OF LONDON.

Fricker's Voice

I am obliged to be here early in the morning. Dawn has barely cracked the sky. I am obliged to be here in my overcoat, because the quaintly clad warders of this place, converted by the ironies of time from warriors to dollies, will in no time be swinging back the dumb and ancient gates and ushering in a flood of gawping tourists. Tower Green. Tower Green, where blood once flowed in such profusion, is now a resting place for lolly sticks and potato crisp bags. Well, we must sell something, mustn't we, even if it is our souls? But I invite you to contemplate with me, if you are able, what this particular fortress represents, for it is a fortress and not a part of Disneyland, as victims of our transatlantic culture might be forgiven for thinking. The bricks are real; tap them and they are not plastic. No, it is not for nothing there are dungeons and execution chambers in this place, not for nothing the block so nearly situated to the Stock Exchange, for we are an executing people, ruthless in authority and merciless in revenge. Roger Casement, converted by the comedy of time from squalid traitor to hero of his race, looked from that window on his fate. The Earl of Essex, a man much loved by crowds, by commoners and artisans, whose name was doubtless chalked by apprentices on walls, suffered here the ultimate, and all the yelling could not blunt the axe. Such is the destiny of those who vaunt themselves above the government. This is a nation which kills all its usurpers, and all the gaudy trash of souvenirs should not blind us to it.

Scene Four

The banqueting hall. An atmosphere of growing drunkenness. FRICKER, *uneasy but game, is standing on his chair. The* SAVAGES *are singing and clapping to 'I Love, You Love'.*

FRICKER.   It must be said — in my defence — I was not informed of the requirement — to perform — in this extraordinary fashion — here tonight — *(The clapping builds up.* FRICKER *begins jerking his hips in a parody of a stripper, slipping his jacket over his shoulders.)* I am not often given — to the extremes of female impersonation — *(Cheers as it falls to the floor. He loosens his tie.)* I would go — so far as to suggest — *(He waves it in the air. Drops it. The* SAVAGES *cheer.)* for all my love of self-expression I am not the most — voluptuous — *(Removing his braces, his trousers fall to his ankles. The* SAVAGES *whistle.)* of creatures — having concentrated more on intellectual exposure — than physical —

DEVOID.   **Shuddup.**

FRICKER *(unbuttons his shirt).*   So what I have to offer tonight — is a rare privilege — *(He twirls his shirt round, to yells of delight, flings it away, pretends to cup his breasts.)*

DEVOID.   **Shuddup.**

FRICKER *(to* CLENCH*).*   Mr President, far be it from me to show an unnatural modesty, but I —

DEVOID. **Get on with it!**

FRICKER. That's all very well —

CLENCH *(standing, clapping).* I think Mr Fricker has acquitted himself with —

MILMO. Hear, hear!

CLENCH. With commendable —

DEVOID. **Get on with it!**

COSTALL. **Starkers!**

FRICKER. Have you not suffered enough?

CLENCH. No — No —

FRICKER. I have missed my vocation, I can see . . .

DEVOID. **Get on with it!**

CLENCH. Sportingly played, Mr Fricker!

FRICKER *(getting down to a chorus of boos).* I am not a novice among connoisseurs. *(Cheers and boos.)*

FRICKER *(slipping his jacket on).* Gentlemen, Gentlemen, I prefer to arouse you in a somewhat less flamboyant manner — has anybody seen my trousers?

DEVOID. **Come on!**

FRICKER. If I must —

COSTALL. **More! More!**

FRICKER. Listen — Listen —

DEVOID. **More! More!**

FRICKER. This is rather good, though I say so myself —

DEVOID. **More!**

FRICKER. If I must have you hard — I would have you hard about the brain! I would have you hard-hearted, and hard-faced!

MILMO. Hear! hear!

CLENCH. A big hand now — please — show our appreciation in the usual way — *(Someone tosses a packet of cigarettes.)* Not that way, thank you, Andrew —

DEVOID. The usual way, you said —

CLENCH. That may well be, but — *(*FRICKER *sits down, lights a cigarette.)* A great sportsman. A great Englishman. *(Applause and stamping.)*

SHISH. I have seen everything. I am prepared to die . . .

TOON. The brandy, Roy.

SHISH. His haunches, grey with loneliness. And his never-fondled knees . . .

TOON. They want the brandy.

SHISH. I could not have teased him. My flashing sequins would not light his poor, dead eyes.

BLINTER. The decanters, please!

CLENCH. Expertly managed, Mr Fricker, if I might venture an opinion.

FRICKER. I am nothing if not daring.

CLENCH. Of course. And therein lies your popularity, I suppose. The public responds to a man who sticks his neck out. Do you agree?

FRICKER. By and large, I think they do.

CLENCH.   They seem, if I gauge the feeling properly, to be in a state of
     expectation. They seem, and I wander the streets a great deal, to be look-
     ing for the Man Who's Not Afraid. I may be wrong, but they are waiting
     for somebody. *(Pause.* FRICKER *expels some smoke.)*
FRICKER.   What are you saying, Mr —
CLENCH.   Clench.
FRICKER.   — Clench?
CLENCH.   I have a company. I make bronze castings. And I don't feel any
     of the parties speaks for me. And I'm not alone in my feeling of desper-
     ation. I'm not alone in thinking what I think.
FRICKER.   What do you think? *(Pause.* CLENCH *looks at him.)*
CLENCH.   Wait and see. *(Pause.* FRICKER *looks at him with a faint hint
     of suspicion. Suddenly* DEVOID, *advanced in inebriation, shoves back
     his chair and stands.)*
DEVOID.   **I'm doing it.** *(There is a burst of applause.)* I'm doing my
     housewife at half past three. *(Cheers. He staggers onto the table, rocks
     slightly as he tries to keep balance. Cries of impatience.)* Wait, will yer?
     *(The noise abates. He slides to his knees, undoes his shirt, and then slips
     his hand underneath.)* You don't waste much time, do you? Oh! *(He
     moves his hand around.)* Look, my husband is — *(Laughter)* Incredibly
     possessive — I — Oh! *(His hand pulls the shirt away.)* Now, look! Oh! Do
     you think my nipples are too large? *(Laughter.)* Oh, thank you, oh, you
     like them, you like them, I don't think — *(He places his hand over his
     crutch. Cheers.)* Take me upstairs! Quickly, upstairs, darling, **upstairs!**
     *(He stamps his feet on the floor, as if going upstairs. Cries and yells. He
     lies back now.)* Pull the curtains, just let me pull the curtains — Stop! The
     curtains, stop! *(He sits up with a jerk.)* Now, look! Don't be so bloody
     rough with me! *(Pause.)* Please, darling. Say you love my nipples. Say
     you — **ow, that hurt!** *(Cheers and laughter. A bread roll is thrown.)* I'm
     so sorry, I'm so sorry, don't be angry with me, I'm so sorry. I'm just not
     used to being — being — being —
LEATHERS ET AL.   **Fucked!**

With a groan, DEVOID *tosses from side to side. Someone sprays him with
soda. A roar of applause. Suddenly he sits up.*

DEVOID.   **Who's that?**
MILMO.   The cat!
DEVOID.   Only the cat . . . only the cat . . . *(He lies down again, starts
     breathing heavily.)* Say you love me, say you love me, say you — *(He sits
     up again, with a jolt.)* **What's that?**
MILMO.   The canary. *(Laughter. He lies back.)*
DEVOID.   The canary . . . only the canary . . . say you love me . . . say you
     love me . . . say you —
COSTALL/PULVERIST.   **I hate your guts!** *(Cheers and bread
     throwing.)*
DEVOID.   Thank you . . . thank you . . . thank you . . . *(He is hit with soda
     water again. He sits up, angrily.)* Look, how can I concentrate! **How can
     I concentrate?** *(Pause. The ribaldry dies down.)* Thank you. *(He goes
     back into character. He lies down on one side, relaxed.)* Can't you stay?

Can't you stay a little bit? Shall I make you a cup of tea? I do like you. Do you like me?

MILMO.   **I hate the sight of you.**

DEVOID *(jerking upright).*   **I said shuddup, didn't I? I said shuddup.**

CLENCH.   All right, Andy.

MILMO.   Shut up and put your knickers on. *(Laughter.)*

DEVOID.   **Belt up or I will come and knock you out.**

CLENCH.   Andy, we have a guest.

DEVOID.   All right, all right, I apologise. I do. I apologise. Just let me finish, then, all right? *(He glares at* MILMO.*)* Just let me finish it. *(Pause. He lies back again. In the silence* BLINTER *is pouring brandies.)* You can ring me. If you feel like it. Any time during the day up until four. I collect the kids at four. The kids come home. If I'm out shopping, try again. Do try again. *(Pause.)* I'm sorry if I wasn't . . . if I didn't . . . if I couldn't . . . sorry . . . sorry . . . *(Pause. He is weeping.)*

CLENCH *(to* FRICKER*).*   The feeling here tonight is that England needs a change.

DEVOID *(getting up to great applause).*   Something like that . . . *(Chatter and drinking continues.)*

SKARDON *(watching* DEVOID *stagger to his chair).*   Andy has been through five marriages.

GREENO.   He looks like a man who will drink himself to a well-earned death . . .

LEATHERS.   He gives me all of his novels. I don't think I've read one of 'em.

SKARDON.   Reading's not your line, Norman.

LEATHERS.   They're all about fucking.

SKARDON.   He says they are about eternal truths.

LEATHERS.   Fucking.

SKARDON *(turning to* GREENO.*)*   Pity your father couldn't come. He always does an imitation of a woman accosted by a drunk. Do you know it?

GREENO.   He doesn't perform a lot at home.

SKARDON.   I love it. Don't you love it, Norman?

GREENO.   I thought of standing in for him. I do something called Girl Exposing Herself.

LEATHERS.   Suits me.

GREENO.   Good, isn't it?

LEATHERS *(going to thump the table).*   I'll call on you.

GREENO.   No! Not yet. Not ready yet.

SKARDON.   Help you if you had a bit more to drink.

GREENO.   I don't want a drink. *(They look appalled.)* I am doing it without a drink.

LEATHERS.   This is the annual dinner, son.

GREENO.   So I see.

LEATHERS.   Then 'ave a drink. *(He shakes his head.)* Don't like liquor. Don't like dogs. Who'd 'ave thought Charlie Greeno would've bulled a prig? *(Pause.* SKARDON *turns to* GREENO.*)*

SKARDON.   Don't mind Norman.

GRENO.   As if you could . . .

SKARDON.   Tonight will go down in the history books. People will talk about tonight, and make false claims that they were here. They will date their lives by it. *(Pause.* SKARDON *looks seriously at* GREENO.*)*

GREENO.   Why?

SKARDON.   It will be like Laurence Olivier said at Agincourt. A rather special day.

GREENO.   This is the annual knicker-fouling isn't it?

SKARDON.   I am so sorry Charlie couldn't be here. The multinationals aren't well represented.

CLENCH *(striking the table ceremoniously).*   **Savages, demons, honourable and ancient outlaws, fellow miscreants, sinister and sordid clique, order, order, please!**

SKARDON *(to* GREENO*).*   Listen. Listen, now.

CLENCH.   I call Ron Pulverist.

SKARDON *(to* GREENO*).*   Ron is a lawyer.

CLENCH.   **Ron Pulverist.** *(A pause, then* PULVERIST *stands, swaying.)*

GREENO.   A pissed lawyer . . .   *(Pause.)*

PULVERIST.   I love my country. All Savages must love their country. If you do not love your country . . . get out of the Savages! *(Pause. He totters, then falls into his seat.)*

SKARDON.   Oh, bleeding hell . . .

CLENCH.   Ron? What's the matter with Ron?

DEVOID *(getting to his feet).*   I will say what Ron was trying to say, shall I?

CLENCH.   No thank you, Andy —

DEVOID.   **Speak for Ron.**

CLENCH.   Will someone tell us what's wrong down there? Is he —

DEVOID *(on his feet).*   **I cannot get my work into print because I'm not a communist.**

CLENCH.   Just sit down, Andy —

DEVOID.   **Fact.**

CLENCH *(to* MILMO*).*   Monty, will you a look at Ron and —

DEVOID.   **A fucking fact.**

LEATHERS.   Siddown.

MILMO *(looking at* PULVERIST*).*   He's gone to sleep.

CLENCH.   Well, can you —

DEVOID.   There are **two themes in art.**

CLENCH.   Andrew, would you be so kind as —

DEVOID *(fingers raised).*   **Two themes.**

CLENCH.   As to —

DEVOID.   One. **Love.** Two. **Death.**

CLENCH *(to* FRICKER*).*   I really must apologise for all — *(*FRICKER *waves a hand complacently, lighting another cigarette.)*

MILMO *(slapping* PULVERIST *softly round the face).*   Ron. Ron.

DEVOID.   **Love and Death.**

COSTALL.   Just sit down, Andy.

DEVOID.   **I will not sit down. Tell him to sit down.** *(He indicates* BLINTER.*)*

COSTALL.   He is a waiter, Andrew.

MILMO *(to* CLENCH*)*.   I'm afraid he's out. Ron's out.

CLENCH *(stricken)*.   Ah . . .

DEVOID.   Now if I was a communist, a four-eyed intellectual fucking **communist** —

SKARDON *(to* GREENO*)*.   This is going wrong.

GREENO.   Oh, is it?

SKARDON.   Horribly wrong.

CLENCH.   Can I — I think —

SKARDON.   I move Andy resumes his seat.

COSTALL.   Seconded.

DEVOID *(to* BLINTER*)*.   **I said siddown.** *(*LEATHERS *and* MILMO *go to assist* DEVOID *into his seat.* DEVOID *grabs a decanter and threatens to toss it across the room.* BLINTER *ducks.)*

BLINTER.   I am not to 'ave things chucked at me!

SKARDON.   Oh, God. Oh, bloody God.

BLINTER.   **Do you 'ear me? I am not to 'ave things chucked at me.**

SKARDON.   Of course not. Of course not.

BLINTER.   **Behave. Fuckin' behave!**

FRICKER *(to* CLENCH*)*.   I wonder if now is not the moment I should take my leave? I did promise Mrs Fricker I should not be late.

SKARDON *(rising)*.   Gentlemen, Gentlemen, we are losing face!

CLENCH.   Hear, hear!

SKARDON.   Ancient order as we are, steeped in public service, let us not squander out dignity!

CLENCH *(clapping)*.   Hear, hear! *(There is a perceptible silence.* SKARDON *looks for words.)* Go on . . . go on, then . . .

SKARDON.   Out of rude beginnings has come many a fair scheme. *(He looks round the hall.)* I was not elected to speak for us tonight, but if it should accord with — *(He looks to* CLENCH *who nods violently.)* — if I am authorised to — *(He nods and nods.)*

CLENCH.   Just get on with it. *(Pause.)*

SKARDON.   Mr Fricker, England is a horse without a rider. Take the reins. *(Pause.* FRICKER *draws on his cigarette.)* This order was among the first to welcome a usurping king onto the sands three hundred years ago. A Savage it was helped King Billy through the surf. Mr. Fricker, when England calls us, we are brisk.

CLENCH.   Hear, hear *(*SKARDON *sits.)* Is that it?

COSTALL.   Have you finished, Ralph? *(*SKARDON *stares at the table.)* So much for the legal fraternity.

CLENCH *(to* COSTALL*)*.   Brian? For the small businessman?

FRICKER *(intimately, to* CLENCH*)*.   What do you make it? Mine says half past twelve.

COSTALL *(standing, pausing)*.   I am a mug.

FRICKER.   I must be fast.

COSTALL.   I am a mug. *(Pause.* FRICKER *adjusts his watch.)* I am a mug because I am a manufacturer. *(Pause.)* A what? **A manufacturer.** *(Pause.)* That's right. I actually make things. *(Pause.)* Bloody hell. And you thought they only made things in Japan. *(Pause.)* Mr Fricker, I am the last Englishman in thermos flasks. *(*GREENO *is unable to resist an*

audible laugh.) **It's not funny! What is so funny about it?** *(*GREENO
bites his lip.) Mr Fricker, I have shed staff like some people rake out
scurf. But I cannot make the things myself. And now they're scratching
for a union. Don't I have enough trouble with the Japanese? I thought we
won the war. Mr Fricker, who was it won the war? I thought we did —
CLENCH.   Brian —
COSTALL.   Didn't we win the war?
CLENCH.   Brian —
COSTALL.   You should see my margins! My starving bloody margins!
CLENCH.   Thank you, Brian. Norman? *(*COSTALL *sits.* LEATHERS
   stands.)
FRICKER *(to* CLENCH*).*   There is a bus at 47 minutes past.
LEATHERS.   I have a dream.
CLENCH *(to* FRICKER*).*   Can't you take a taxi?
FRICKER.   I have never used one.
LEATHERS.   Well, I call it a dream . . .
CLENCH.   Never used a taxi?
FRICKER.   I am perfectly content to go by bus.
CLENCH.   But —
LEATHERS.   I call it a dream, but actually I think it's a memory. Of a fat
   copper on a bicycle. And of a kiddie nicking apples. Scrumping, I think it's
   called. A fat copper, slapping a schoolkid's arse. *(Pause.)* My arse.
CLENCH *(in dismay to* SKARDON*).*   Ezra wants to go and catch a bus.
   *(*SKARDON *looks horrified.)*
LEATHERS.   Last week one of my sergeants had his eye knocked out.
   Someone exercising his right to demonstration hit him with an engineering
   brick. Before they got it off the road one of the horses trod on it.
SKARDON.   A bus?
LEATHERS.   What is 'appening in our streets?
SKARDON.   A bus?
DEVOID.   **I will talk about the Arts.**
CLENCH.   No thank you, Andy —
DEVOID.   **I am the last great English novelist!**
FRICKER *(to* CLENCH*).*   I am never out of doors after twelve o'clock.
CLENCH.   Mr Fricker, I don't think you have heard us yet.
FRICKER.   I think I have absorbed the gist.
SKARDON *(to* CLENCH*).*   He's not to go.
CLENCH.   Perhaps we haven't been as clear as we —
SKARDON.   He's not to go.
CLENCH.   All right! *(He turns back to* FRICKER*.)* Mr Fricker, it's the crown
   of England we are offering tonight.
FRICKER.   Thank you, but I believe someone is already wearing it.
CLENCH.   That was a metaphor.
FRICKER.   Indeed. *(He stands up.)* Gentlemen —
DEVOID.   **My trilogy has yet to find a publisher!**
FRICKER.   Gentlemen, I am afraid you will consider me ungrateful if I
   presume to lecture you. It is, after all, somewhat late in the evening to embark
   on a discussion of the constitution —
LEATHERS.   Fuck the constitution.

FRICKER.   Yes, well, I rather gathered the prevailing sentiment to be of that order here tonight —

COSTALL.   Save the nation, Ezra!

FRICKER.   Nothing would give me greater pleasure, but I must return —

DEVOID.   **Look. You are the loud boy. You are the only loud boy we have got. I don't like you. I think you are a pedantic fart. But you are the loud boy. So get on with it.** *(To a chorus of approval he falls into his seat.)*

FRICKER.   You shower me with compliments. In return, I would shower you with wisdom. *(They are noisy and restless.)* Gentlemen, the constitution is the best armour for your privilege. *(He looks round the room. A missile strikes him.)* I have a bus.

He leaves the table to a mounting din. SKARDON watches as he walks the length of the hall and tries the handle of the doors. They are locked.

SKARDON *(to* GREENO*)*.   I told you this would be a bit of history . . .

FRICKER.   The doors are locked. *(Everyone is looking at him.)* The doors are locked.

CLENCH.   Only by a unanimous resolution of the order can the gate be opened. Statutes of the Savages.

FRICKER.   Would you kindly expedite the necessary business? The driver of the night bus is not famed for sticking to the timetable.

CLENCH.   That the assembly be dissolved. Proposer please? *(No one speaks.)*

FRICKER.   I propose it.

LEATHERS.   I don't think you're bona fide, Mr Fricker.

FRICKER.   I am the guest of honour.

CLENCH.   Quite. That the assembly be dissolved. Proposer, please? *(Silence.)* The motion falls. *(Laughter.)*

FRICKER *(from the end of the hall.)*.   I don't think you understand. It is a matter of principle with me that I am not abroad after twelve o'clock. I believe profoundly in the doctrine of the early night.

MILMO.   Let's talk about the nation, Ezra.

FRICKER.   I am a member of parliament. It is contempt of parliament to hold a member in a place against his will. *(Pause.)* You can be tried at the bar of the House. *(Pause.)* It is treason. *(Pause.)* The penalties are most severe for this!

PULVERIST.   Rex versus Crichton, Bowyer, Shanks and Oats, 1820.

CLENCH.   Oh, Ron's awake . . .

FRICKER *(turning to* SHISH*)*.   Would you be so kind as to inform a constable that I am in need of assistance? There is one on the door of the Rhodesian consulate. *(*SHISH *stares at him).* Get along. *(He just stares.)* Will you? *(*SHISH *doesn't move. After a pause, he turns, walks back to his place at the table. There is a burst of cheering and table thumping. He sits, lights a cigarette. Pause.)* Well, I have often been called a cat among the pigeons. I have never been a pigeon among the cats before. *(Renewed cheering.* PULVERIST *stands, leaning on his fists on the table.)*

PULVERIST.   There are times a man, no matter how great and perspicacious, needs to be reminded of his responsibilities. In no uncertain manner. If he won't take the burden on himself, he finds it thrust upon him. *(Cries of 'Hear, Hear!')*

SKARDON.   Roy comes through drink like a man in fog. Lost one minute, daylight the next.

PULVERIST.   Mr Fricker, we have kidnapped you for England. *(Cheers. He falls into his seat. Drinks.)*

FRICKER.   Well, I am comforted to know my suffering is for the nation: a word that knows no rest! And like all words, likely to be annexed by the unscrupulous. When I hear it uttered, I tremble for its reputation. Does nobody care what company it keeps?

LEATHERS.   What is nation, Mr Fricker?

FRICKER.   Well, I am a good academic. I am better at telling you what it is not, and to arrive at what it is by a process of elimination. But I doubt you have the patience for all that.

COSTALL.   What is it, Ezra?

FRICKER.   Well, I have just —

COSTALL.   What is it, though?

FRICKER.   It is what separates us from everybody else. It is our smell. It is the flavour of our breath.

COSTALL.   It's not foreigners, is it?

FRICKER.   It is not foreigners, no.

MILMO.   They are out to kill the nation, Mr Fricker.

FRICKER.   I cannot see what this has got to do with causing me to miss my bus. *(Groans.)*

MILMO.   He is so very *faux naif*.

DEVOID.   The virgin playing hard to get.

CLENCH.   We think it has this to do with it. The people say you are the last Englishman. For you they will come out and frolic in the streets. For you, they'll drag themselves out of the betting shop. Until tonight, you were the hero of a mob. But we aren't a mob, are we, gentlemen?

MILMO.   We are. We are the governing mob. *(Pause.* FRICKER *looks at them.)*

CLENCH.   Ralph, show Mr. Fricker the top hat. *(*SKARDON *reaches under the table. Takes out a top hat.)* Say yes to us, and we will pass around that hat. And at the end, there will be cheques lining it like straws in a bird's nest. Who knows what the nest will hatch? We are holding dinners in every city in the land. *(Pause.)*

FRICKER.   You are offering me a party.

CLENCH.   We have a programme. For the nation.

FRICKER.   Do you?

CLENCH.   Call the party what you like. I rather fancied progress in the title, but Brian likes Salvation. Do you like Salvation?

FRICKER.   Salvation?

LEATHERS.   Makes me think of tarts in bonnets.

FRICKER.   I have to do my duty, as I see it. I cannot say I should have acted, but did not.

MILMO.   Oh, no, indeed.

FRICKER.   I cannot say, power was given me, but I used it not.

SAVAGES.   No, no.

FRICKER.   I cannot say, I was in one party but they would not heed me. Therefore I went and hid my face.

COSTALL.   Absolutely not, Ezra.

FRICKER.   In my raiment closed me in.

SAVAGES.   No, no.

FRICKER.   But rather I should say, the people laid their finger on me and I could not say no!

SKARDON.   Could not say no.

FRICKER.   I was called and could not cover up my ears!

PULVERIST.   Spot on, Ezra!

FRICKER.   I went forth —

SAVAGES.   Went forth —

FRICKER.   Gathering my weapons on my way! Some fine, some not so fine —

SAVAGES.   Some not so fine —

FRICKER.   But fashioned to the task!

SAVAGES.   The task! The task, Ezra!

PULVERIST.   Give him the funds!

COSTALL.   Give 'im the money, Mabel!

DEVOID.   Come on, love!

LEATHERS.   Pass the hat!

MILMO.   The hat!

LEATHERS.   The hat!

GREENO, *taking the hat, climbs onto the table and begins a striptease. The diners reprise 'I Love, You Love'.*

FRICKER *(dazzled)*.   I have to — I have to —

COSTALL *(chequebook in hand)*.   The hat!

FRICKER.   My place — in — history —

CLENCH.   Of course. *(His jaw works. More diners stand, shout. Cheques are dropped into the hat.)*

MILMO.   To flog a metaphor to death, we were afraid you'd missed the bus. Some would have it you had missed the bus.

FRICKER.   I am the spirit of the English race . . .

CLENCH.   The only trouble with the spirit of the English race is it can be scattered by a dozen mounted police . . .

SKARDON.   Give him the money!

MILMO.   They want the hat. Give 'em the hat!

CLENCH.   Your chance, Ezra.

FRICKER.   **I have to know what history will say of me!**

LEATHERS.   I will tell you what History will say. History will say I have given that man too many opportunities.

COSTALL.   Power comes out of the barrel of a fountain pen! My cheque! My cheque! How many noughts?

DEVOID.   Four noughts!

COSTALL.   This is the company account!

LEATHERS.   Five noughts!

CLENCH.   I thought Brian was bankrupt . . .

FRICKER.   I can't think clearly after twelve o'clock . . .

CLENCH.   Mr Fricker, does this not have the smack of History?

MILMO.   I write — I write — five hundred pounds!

LEATHERS.   Five hundred pounds?

MILMO.   Five hundred pounds!

LEATHERS.   You get that for one bloody Arab's hysterecomy!

MILMO.   Where's the hat?

DEVOID *(looking at* FRICKER*).*   Pay him the money! Look at him swelling like a cock!

SKARDON.   Give him some, then, Andrew.

DEVOID.   I am giving him some! I have nothing, but I am giving him some.

CLENCH.   Cough up for England! Dig deep for your children, lads!

LEATHERS *(staring in horror at* GREENO's *naked breasts).*   Christ — the boy's a tart.

GREENO.   I am making a statement.

SKARDON *(staggered).*   Miles . . . Miles . . .

LEATHERS.   It is not Miles yer stupid git!

SKARDON.   Miles . . .

GREENO *(holding a paper).*   **I am making a statement!**

CLENCH.   I examined for tit! You saw me! I examined for tit!

MILMO.   I think I shall be ill . . .

GREENO.   **Women are everywhere. Women are universal.**

MILMO.   Cover it up! Cover it up!

GREENO.   **The historical conspiracy of the male to exclude the female from the functioning of power has been exposed** — *(*COSTALL *seizes the paper out of her hand.)* Give me my paper!

MILMO.   Somebody cover her up . . .! *(*COSTALL *tears up her statement.)*

GREENO.   You have no r:ght to take my property! *(She is sprayed from a soda syphon. She improvises.)* We are going to assume — our proper place — the oppression of women by — male fascism — will not — *(She is hit by food and drink.)* **You are vile bastards!** *(A cheer goes up.)*

DEVOID.   You got no tit.

GREENO.   I will not be moved — from here — I —

DEVOID.   **Got — no — tit.**

SKARDON *(to* CLENCH*).*   What is the procedure for this?

GREENO.   My father is a **chauvinist — big business — fascist —**

DEVOID.   You are not a woman. I deny you are a woman.

GREENO.   I deny you are a novelist. You are a literary prostitute!

PULVERIST *(to the* WAITERS, *who watch impassively).*   I have two fivers says you wouldn't mind dumping Miss Greeno in the street.

BLINTER.   They do, do they? *(He doesn't move.)*

PULVERIST.   All right, then, three.

BLINTER.   I am a waiter. Not a bouncer.

SKARDON *(standing, in the racket).*   Susan . . . Susan . . .

GREENO *(turning on him).*   Don't bring your patrician grease to me!

SKARDON.   You have betrayed your father's trust —

GREENO.   You cannot betray evil! Only liberate the truth!

SKARDON.   Miles will be ashamed of you!

GREENO.   **Miles is in this with me! All the way!** *(*SKARDON *sits wearily in his seat. The abuse and shouting reach a climax.)* **Ezra Fricker! You are a frightened, vicious little man! You will be —** *(*COSTALL *and others go to*

*pull her down.)*Do not touch me! I have not finished my statement! Do not touch me! *(They go to grab her.)*
BLINTER.   Don't touch her!   *(They look at him.)* Let her go.

He holds out her trousers and jacket. The room falls silent. GREENO takes the clothes, climbs down from the table. She walks the length of the banqueting hall, then stops at the doors.

GREENO.   I think the doors are locked.

Pause. CLENCH dips in his pocket for the keys. He tosses them to her; they slide along the floor. She unlocks the doors, goes out, slams them behind her. FRICKER watches, then rises and exits in silence. Suddenly, No. 38 Air, 'Why Do The Nations?'

Blackout.

ACT TWO

Scene One

A Berkshire Garden, 1945. FRICKER *is sitting in a deckchair. He is wearing uniform, officer's cap and overcoat. After some moments, he stands, staring as someone approaches. His face falls.* CRYSTAL, *advanced in pregnancy, comes up to him. Pause.*

FRICKER. You are pregnant. By another man.

CRYSTAL. You are alive. By a fluke. *(Pause. He swallows hard.)*

FRICKER. May I enquire whose child it is?

CRYSTAL. My husband's.

FRICKER. Backlawn's?

CRYSTAL. Yes.

FRICKER. But Backlawn is an idiot. By your own reckoning.

CRYSTAL. Yes . . . *(Pause.)* Yes.

FRICKER. Then why nourish the seed of idiots? Are there not enough idiots but you want to propogate them? *(Pause.)* Forgive me, but I am —

CRYSTAL. Furious?

FRICKER. The letters I wrote you. The pentameters. From every place the army stopped.

CRYSTAL. I'm afraid I don't read Greek. *(Pause.)*

FRICKER. Mrs Backlawn, may I tell you something? I have borne you in my heart from Normandy to Luneburg. You have swum before my eyes in squealing jeeps and on the roofs of sodden canvasses. I could not look into my frozen shaving water but I saw you there. After three years I come back and I find this. I have to tell you I feel robbed. *(Pause.)* Give me my postcards, please.

CRYSTAL. Wasn't it fun in the commandos?

FRICKER. I hope you won't succumb to the temptation of the minute. I hope you will not mock.

CRYSTAL. I'm trying. Believe me, I am.

FRICKER. I was not in the commandos. I was in intelligence.

CRYSTAL. Oh yes. *(Pause.)* Intelligence . . . *(She begins to laugh.)*

FRICKER. What is so amusing about intelligence?

CRYSTAL *(stifling her laughter).* Nothing . . .

FRICKER. I see your condition renders you prey to senseless laughter. Perhaps you should take advantage of the seat —

CRYSTAL *(giggling).* No —

FRICKER. The deckchair is at your disposal — *(He goes to take her arm. She pulls away.)*

CRYSTAL. No! *(Pause. She glares at him.)* Who in fuck's name do you think you are? How dare you, you beribboned little snot! *(He is transfixed by horror. Pause.)* Pregnant women do not like deckchairs. We get in and then we can't get out again. The centre of gravity, you see, shifts to the front . . . *(Pause.)* How are you planning to enjoy the peace?

FRICKER. I feel sure my career is of negligible interest to you —

CRYSTAL. Come on! *(Pause.)*

FRICKER. I have been accepted as a parliamentary candidate.

CRYSTAL. For whom?

FRICKER. The Conservative and Unionist party. *(Pause.)*

CRYSTAL. Backlawn and I are communists.

FRICKER. The war has seen some strange shifts in allegiances.

CRYSTAL. From cock to communism in one fell swoop.

FRICKER. I feel sure the doyens of private enterprise can only be relieved to learn your husband has added his considerable intellectual weight to the opposition —

CRYSTAL. Silly.

FRICKER. I feel sure this news will enable them to sleep at nights —

CRYSTAL. Silly.

FRICKER. Backlawn is a communist! What is Berkshire coming to?

CRYSTAL. He is a crack shot with a 303. I don't think he aspires to the leadership. *(Pause.* FRICKER *looks earnestly at her.)*

FRICKER. Am I not attractive to you any more?

CRYSTAL. Well, since you ask —

FRICKER. I have never forgotten that evening when I might have seen you naked by the light of London's fires.

CRYSTAL. Not naked.

FRICKER. No?

CRYSTAL. A bit undressed. It takes time to be naked. *(Pause.)* Look, I think you ought to know I am a different woman.

FRICKER. Of course.

CRYSTAL. I do mean different. I know it has been a fad and fetish to go about proclaiming metamorphosis. The war has been an impostors' paradise. No time to look beneath the skin. But I am sick to the stomach with girls in bus queues saying they are trying out the new morality. The only new morality is to get old England off our backs.

FRICKER. You have taken to the party with a vengeance.

CRYSTAL. I am not a slave to orgasm. I have done it, and I can honestly say I'd rather curl up with a book.

FRICKER. I see.

CRYSTAL. I wonder if you do.

FRICKER. No doubt you will scale my eyes . . .

CRYSTAL. I am saying for those brief seconds on the grass I paid a very heavy price. The complete subjection of my intellect. I actually believed as long as I was fucking I was living. Lies. Changing is living. Changing the world. *(Pause.)*

FRICKER. I have come to the wrong address. I have come shopping in the wrong store.

CRYSTAL. **You are not listening!**

FRICKER. I am listening.

CRYSTAL. All right, why don't you hear?

FRICKER. Ah. That is altogether different. *(Pause.)* I wrote my poems to an enigmatic lady. I do not see the enigmatic lady here.

CRYSTAL. Oh, God, the burdens you stagger under . . .

FRICKER *(picking up his cap).* Have you my postcards please?

CRYSTAL.   No. I'm afraid I chucked then in the bin. To be absolutely truthful
    I didn't know who Ezra was. That is the problem with enigmatic women.
    They forget who had them last.
FRICKER.   Well, perhaps I shall have more luck in politics. I was wrong to
    wander from the path of legitimacy. You are a married woman, after all.
    There is a lesson there. And as you say, a man should not let passion stand in
    the way of his career.
CRYSTAL.   I never said that.
FRICKER.   Oh, didn't you? I shall look for a woman of simplicity. A woman
    who will put me in good stead.
CRYSTAL.   Well, naturally. *(Pause. He looks at her.)*
FRICKER.   I must say, I find you beautiful. But you are my final aberration. I
    am 25. *(There is a shot.)* What's that?
CRYSTAL.   Backlawn shooting.
FRICKER.   Shooting?
CRYSTAL.   I shouldn't let him see the uniform.
FRICKER *(alarmed).*   Is there no way out of the garden?
CRYSTAL.   You're afraid!
FRICKER.   I did not fight my way through Europe only to die in Berkshire at
    the hands of a renegade stockbroker. What is across that fence?
CRYSTAL.   The workers have you on the run!
FRICKER.   I will not stay to quarrel with your terminology. *(He begins to
    climb the fence.)*
CRYSTAL.   I loathe everything you stand for.
FRICKER.   I am not defeated. I am making a tactical retreat.
CRYSTAL.   Roger! There is a soldier on the fence!
FRICKER.   Do not be ridiculous!
CRYSTAL.   **Rapid fire!** *(FRICKER drops out of sight. His head reappears.)*
FRICKER.   I ask you to consider the next twenty-five years. Which of us will
    be carried higher by the turning of the wheel of History, and which of us sunk
    in the mud.
CRYSTAL.   History is not a wheel. It is linear, and it leads straight to the
    Socialist Republic. Now, shove off! *(FRICKER drops, walks away up the
    lane.* CRYSTAL *watches his figure disappear.)* Because he is funny does not
    mean we shouldn't be afraid of him. Fear the comic. Laugh, but hold the
    knife . . .

Scene Two

*The House of Commons. A room, historic and occasional. Deep leather arm
chairs. A long, antique table. A* SERVANT *stands by the door. A body of MPs
enter, straggling, gossiping.*

CAMBERLEY.   I will sit there, Norris, my love. For my back.
PINCER.   Sit anywhere? Elizabeth?
CAMBERLEY.   Thank you. I have a persistent pain.
PINCER.   Well, there's a view!
BAKER.   I came in here in 1966.

SATCHLEY.   You must be the only one —

BAKER.   I am, I think.

CAMBERLEY.   The only what?

BAKER.   Who was in Alec's cabinet.

PINCER.   Are we all in?

SATCHLEY *(to the* SERVANT*).*   There are five of us.

PINCER.   Are we all in? *(The* SERVANT *is counting heads).*

SATCHLEY.   He has to lock the door, you see. Yes, we are all in.

SERVANT.   Five. Five heads.

SACHLEY.   Thank you.

SERVANT.   I will lock it, then.

BAKER.   Is there scotch?

SERVANT.   There is everything, Mr Baker.

SATCHLEY.   Thank you. *(He goes out, locking the door.)*

BAKER *(at the drinks).*   Self service, all right?

SATCHLEY *(sitting).*   I think the quicker we move the better.

CAMBERLEY.   Give us a scotch, Harry.

BAKER.   Self-service, old man.

CAMBERLEY.   Oh, come on!

SATCHLEY.   Everyone to sit down, please.

DOGGITT.   Are you sitting there?

PINCER.   No, I am.

DOGGITT.   Oh.

PINCER.   Sit there if you like.

SATCHLEY.   Can we —

CAMBERLEY.   Bugger.

BAKER.   Do you want soda?

SATCHLEY.   Can we hurry up, please?

BAKER.   Sorry.

SATCHLEY.   Because we want to look decisive.

DOGGITT.   We are decisive.

SACHLEY.   Yes, we want to look it too. Harry — please —

BAKER.   Right.

PINCER.   I never knew this room existed. Did you?

SATCHLEY.   Brian.

CAMBERLEY.   It's a funny thing, is it not —

SATCHLEY.   Boyd, I am calling to order now —

CAMBERLEY.   I know you are, Elizabeth, but I am saying it is a funny thing,
   and I know it is a tradition of the House, I do not care to be reminded, that we
   have just allowed ourselves, at this moment of extreme and utter crisis, to be
   locked into a room no bigger than the Black Hole of Calcutta, the exact
   dimensions of which I do not recall —

DOGGITT.   Eight foot by three —

CAMBERLEY.   I am obliged to you, Norris — by a caretaker, the political
   loyalties of whom we do not know, without a single telephone to connect us
   with the outside world —

PINCER.   It is a tradition —

CAMBERLEY.   I knew someone would want to remind me — I am well aware it is a tradition on choosing a new prime minister during the term of office — that we are locked in this very room — I am saying, to all intents and purposes, we have delivered the government into the hands of a servant of the House. I mention it, that's all.

SATCHLEY.   I am calling the meeting to order.

CAMBERLEY.   All right, you don't think it's funny. I do.

BAKER.   It has always been the way the House —

CAMBERLEY.   Oh, no, Harry, please!

DOGGITT.   Order!

PINCER.   Order!

SATCHLEY.   Thank you. It is a quarter past three. I would like us to have our statement out by half past at the latest.

CAMBERLEY.   Well, nothing like an optimist!

SATCHLEY.   We are saddled with a three-way choice. We have Lionel Bissell. We have Keith Hacker. And we have Ezra Fricker. I need not remind you, need I, that there is no precedent whatsoever for elevating a prime minister directly from the back benches, but —

BAKER.   Oh! Oh!

SATCHLEY.   May I finish? *(Pause.)* But that in itself is no reason for excluding him. Now I want to limit whatever there is likely to be in the way of debate becasue as I just said people will interpret delay as dither and that will cost the new incumbent something in authority. I move we vote.

PINCER.   Seconded.

CAMBERLEY.   Of course not. No.

DOGGITT.   Boyd, the country is waiting.

CAMBERLEY.   I'm sorry. Of course not.

BAKER.   Hear! hear

CAMBERLEY.   You do not move to a vote on a matter of this significance without prior discussion, and I say that even if the country is tottering on its feet and the reds half-way up the staircase —

PINCER.   It is tottering on its feet, and the reds are —

BAKER.   That is contentious —

DOGGITT.   Is it? **Is it?**

BAKER.   That is contentious!

CAMBERLEY.   There is a right of discussion which I intend to uphold, and it cannot be eliminated by a vote.

DOGGITT.   That is technically true.

CAMBERLEY.   Technically true? He says it is technically true! It is actually true! Do not attempt to tarnish my right to free discussion by describing it as technical, I beg you. Habeas Corpus is technical —

DOGGITT.   Absolutely!

CAMBERLEY.   All right — but —

BAKER.   Silly —

CAMBERLEY.   All right, but there are more than a thousand people in the square down there assembled for a man most of you appear to have discounted, and—

SATCHLEY.   No one has discounted anyone —

CAMBERLEY.   Well —

SATCHLEY.   No one has discounted anyone —

CAMBERLEY.   All right, in which case no one legitimately disputes my right of argument, however brief, however circumscribed.

PINCER.   No one is denying your right.

CAMBERLEY.   Well, what is this about a vote?

DOGGITT.   Elizabeth's point, which I think is a right one, is that confidence relies on promptness in this instance, and that every second wasted . . .

CAMBERLEY.   Wasted! You see, you call debate wasted!

DOGGITT.   Can I finish, Boyd, please? I know you are hot on Ezra Fricker —

CAMBERLEY.   Who said I was hot for Fricker? (Groans.) Who said I was? We have not opened the discussion yet. (Groans.)You make my point for me!

BAKER.   I think the British people can be relied upon to show —

PINCER.   Oh, fuck all that —

BAKER.   Well, so you say, but —

SATCHLEY.   We are thinking of pound sterling, Harry. You know — pound sterling?

CAMBERLEY.   I hate to bring the odious whiff of democracy to bear upon this meeting, but we have a duty do we not, to respond to the legitimate aspirations of the people, and —

DOGGITT.   No!

CAMBERLEY.   And there can be no questions, can there —

DOGGITT.   No.

CAMBERLEY.   Of whom —

DOGGITT.   No!

CAMBERLEY.   The man they —

DOGGITT/PINCER.   No! No! (CAMBERLEY shrugs, sits back. Pause.)

DOGGITT.   I move we give Boyd five. All right? Boyd? Five?

FRICKER'S LONDON. ON ST. PAUL'S.

Fricker's Voice

Money and God. The rich man and his deity. The merchant and his temple. St. Paul's Cathedral. Every stone of it raised at the behest of trade, every ornament and scroll, every extravagance of the baroque, paid out of commerce, every brick lifted by usury. The businessman confronts his God. Across the river his well-stocked warehouses. A hundred yards away, the Old Bailey, where they administer his law. At Rotherhithe, his gunboats taking on their stores. Within a square mile of the altar, the tradesman and his wherewithal. Culture and profit. Profit and culture. Handel and the stock exchange. Purcell and the bank rate. The Messiah and the going rate for spice. Choirs and capital, art and accountancy.

Scene Four

The rear of a large car, travelling. FRICKER *is sitting with* DORIS FRICKER *and two* AIDES.

FRICKER.   At the moment of crisis, only one thing matters. Being in the right
    spot. Legions of men whom History might have touched upon the shoulder
    were at their moment discovered lying in their beds or in their mistresses.
    They will not say that of me. I may be on the Great North Road . . .
TUESDAY.   The M1, Mr Fricker.
FRICKER.   The Great North Road; but the telephone links me like a trans-
    fusion to the blood-bottle of Westminster. I have rarely felt such an affection
    for technology.
IMBER *(filing through papers).*   I have a letter from the Department of the
    Environment. They ask what wallpaper you like. Three samples, here. *(He
    holds out tiny paper samples.)*
FRICKER *(dangling them).*   There is a great irony in the contrasting
    efficiencies within a single state. On the one hand, the docks lie idle, weeds
    sprout between the railway lines, and industry manifests the vitality of a
    week-old corpse, and on the other, a servant deep within some ministry, in
    preparation for an eventuality which may not occur, is collecting information
    from all the likely candidates as to their whim in decorating Downing Street. I
    think we take heart from this single enquiry that come what may, the civil
    service will be loyal. Pass them to Doris, please. Doris will be in charge of
    appearances. *(*IMBER *hands the samples over.)* How many other copies of
    that letter went out?
IMBER.   It says —
TUESDAY *(looking over his shoulder).*   Three.
IMBER.   Three.
FRICKER.   Three. I think we can rest assured on whose desks the remaining
    copies lie. And the papers have been speculating about six candidates! If you
    want the truth, if you are after a reasonable assessment, ignore the papers.
    Ask where the decorators are.
TUESDAY.   Hacker and Bissell are in the Commons.
FRICKER.   They would be. It is the nature of the least likely candidates to lean
    against the door. There is no better formula for the man who hopes to bring
    to birth a lifetime's dream than at the moment to be seen, business as usual. It
    is very good for confidence.
TUESDAY.   Hacker cancelled a visit to a missile cruiser.
FRICKER.   It is a cancellation he will regret.
TUESDAY.   I would remind you, Mr. Fricker, if I might, of Trotsky.
IMBER.   I don't think so . . .
FRICKER.   Do remind me of Trotsky. Remind me of anyone. Feel free.
TUESDAY.   Trotsky, who in his casualness, slipped out of history.
FRICKER.   Trotsky was three thousand miles from Moscow. Trotsky was in a
    mood. No wonder Stalin struck. A politician cannot afford moods. Moods
    are for girls and artists.
TUESDAY.   If I may press the point —
FRICKER.   Press away!
TUESDAY.   St. Clare's is thirty miles from Charing Cross.
FRICKER.   There you have it! Thirty miles is twenty minutes in the car.
TUESDAY.   I beg to suggest that is simply arithmetic, that the essence of my
    point is that Trotsky was not in the Supreme Soviet, and you are not in the
    House.

FRICKER.   I know very little of Trotsky. You are the Trotskyite.

TUESDAY.   Forgive me, I was not aiming to educate you —

FRICKER.   Look at the view! It is a tragedy that the strain of modern travel inhibits a proper appreciation of the view . . . *(They look out the window. Pause.)* Where would you have me be? Sitting in the tea-bar of the House, biting my nails? I put it to you, my very absence from the building is the strongest urging for my suit. I am the man for the nation. There are a thousand people chanting my name, in endless monotony, beneath the windows of the House. I do not hear a single voice for Hacker or for Bissell. When the cameras find me, I shall be deep in business. At once, before the cameras, I shall quit, my car will sweep into the city flanked by outriders. It is the way a new leader should enter his capital. Where is the glory in stepping across a corridor? The cameras will barely find the time to focus. But from thirty miles! There is a picture! There is a spectacle for the weary public eye!

IMBER.   There is no denying Ezra's learned a lot from his incursion into television.

FRICKER.   I have learned a trick or two. I have learned that in a crisis the public love an ugly face. Bissell is doomed by his good looks. They will earn him passage into women's bedrooms but never into Downing Street. As for Hacker, everybody knows the man has putty fists. I am the strong man, I am the bruiser.

IMBER.   It is a delight to see a man so confident.

FRICKER.   The problem, if there is a problem, is only this. The cabinet are not my friends. Dare I say it, they are almost, to a woman, my enemies. Every man who votes for me votes himself out of a job. They know when I go to Her Majesty I go with a list of ministers scarcely one of whom has seen the inside of a cabinet room. Nevertheless, I deem it impossible they will reject me. I am the genie in the bottle. If they do not appoint me I will blow my lid, and half of London will be fizzing with me.

IMBER *(looking at his watch).*   They are in session. As from — now.

FRICKER.   When can we expect the phone call? I am accepting bets.

TUESDAY *(unscrewing a flask).*   I have never seen Ezra half as cocky. Have you, Mrs Fricker? Ever seen him quite like this?

FRICKER.   Doris will not be active in the public eye. She will set an example, will you not, my dear, of silent service? To my wife I bequeath all garden fêtes. *(He drinks.)*

TUESDAY *(to DORIS).*   You must be very proud.

DORIS.   Yes. *(Pause.)*

FRICKER.   And here we are. This is the place. St. Clare's. My first duty will be to clamp a preservation order on your venerable red brick. Who will get the relevant department? Do you want it, Dick?

IMBER.   Press are here!

TUESDAY.   I would not say no, Mr Fricker.

FRICKER.   Remind me this time tomorrow. I had earmarked it for Jock McVicar —

IMBER.   Look at the press!

FRICKER *(grinning through the window as if at a crowd).*   But I am no lover of the Scots.

IMBER *(reading)*.   Sir George Fleming —
FRICKER.   I know George —
IMBER.   Will greet you on the upper terrace —

Sound of press and public besieging the car. DORIS *looks at* FRICKER *who is wild eyed with delight.*

FRICKER.   The flood of history! It rocks our boat! *(Cheers and boos.)*

FRICKER'S LONDON. ON CLAPHAM JUNCTION.

Fricker's Voice

I am standing in the midst of a Golgotha. An industrial Golgotha. I am standing in a boneyard of the nineteenth century. Clapham Junction. And here it was in the winter of 1895, there stood a man who, in the manner of geniuses, *pushed his luck*. A man who, accustomed to be feted, felt the spittle of his erstwhile worshippers and heard their din, not in the accolade of dazzled admiration, but in the full throat of contempt. I am speaking of Oscar Wilde, who no doubt at that moment, between two warders, handcuffed and waiting for the prison train, was *dreading Reading*. This dismal junction never witnessed such a savage turning of the wheel of fate, and do its dull timbers not serve to remind us how the fickle public loves nothing better than to see its heroes riding in the dust . . .

Scene Five

The room in the House of Commons. The Cabinet are sprawled wearily around the table.

BAKER.   Drinking too much.
SATCHLEY.   I wonder if we shouldn't have the drinks taken away?
PINCER.   I think some of us are beginning to resort to it.
BAKER.   Well, of course I will. Obviously I will resort to it. That is what liquor's for, resorting to.
DOGGITT.   You see, we have been half an hour now. That is twice what Elizabeth suggested.
CAMBERLEY.   Yes, well I have been urging, haven't I? And not altogether vainly. Urging is a time-consuming business.
DOGGITT.   I am thinking of whoever we choose.
PINCER.   The lucky sod.
DOGGITT.   I am thinking of the delay and the subsequent impression it will make. It will look as though we were divided.
BAKER.   We are divided.
DOGGITT.   It is like a jury. The longer it is out the less convincing the acquittal looks.
BAKER.   I say we are divided and it doesn't matter who knows it.
DOGGITT.   Harry, that is not the tradition of this party, and you know it.
PINCER.   May I come back to Sterling?

CAMBERLEY. No.

PINCER. Because —

BAKER. No.

CAMBERLEY. Brian, we are not discussing a slide in sterling. There would be a slide in sterling if the English Channel turned to oil. We are talking about the last ditch. There are no more ditches after this.

BAKER. Hear, hear.

CAMBERLEY. Which is why I am pressing Fricker. Because sans Fricker, sans every fucking thing.

PINCER. You are about the only person who thinks so.

CAMBERLEY. I am not. I am the only person who **says** so. You are all thinking it —

DOGGITT. I'm not thinking it —

CAMBERLEY. You are all thinking it, but none of you are saying it. But I tell you every clerk and costermonger in the street has got Fricker on his lips.

DOGGITT. I must say there is something very touching in Boyd's deference to — what was it — clerks and costermongers? Perhaps someone should tell him the country is not being governed for clerks and costermongers, or for milkmen, or zoo attendants, for that matter.

BAKER. Thank you, Norris —

DOGGITT. Well, let's get down to business, shall we? I suggest we offer Fricker a senior cabinet post —

CAMBERLEY. Oh!

DOGGITT. I suggest we offer him Employment under Keith.

SATCHLEY. No —

CAMBERLEY. Rubbish.

DOGGITT. Boyd says it's rubbish.

SATCHLEY. It is rubbish.

BAKER. Fricker will not come in under Keith.

SATCHLEY. Absolutely.

DOGGITT. You say so.

SATCHLEY. I do say so.

DOGGITT. And I say if he doesn't it will look peevish and will cost him his support.

CAMBERLEY. Norris —

PINCER. Norris has a point there —

CAMBERLEY. Norris —

PINCER. I was rather expecting to get that post myself —

CAMBERLEY. Norris, you are after demolishing Fricker. You want to dismantle him. That is your affair. Your private affair. You think by giving him that choice you will slip the bolts out and he will fall apart. I say that is not the business of this meeting —

BAKER. Too clever, Norris —

CAMBERLEY. Too clever by half.

PINCER. Where does the Queen stand in all this?

CAMBERLEY. The Queen wants Fricker.

PINCER. You don't know that.

CAMBERLEY. I do know it because without Fricker she will be sitting on her rim in the street. There will be no throne. He is the last hope of the palace guards, I tell you that. The lackeys have his picture under their wigs.

SATCHLEY.   Let's be absolutely clear on one thing. Fricker will have us out. He will have a cabinet of lunatics.

PINCER.   Quite.

CAMBERLEY.   Of course he will. He hates our guts. He is mad. There is no question in my mind that he is mad.

SATCHLEY.   Well, then.

CAMBERLEY.   I say that is an asset. The time for madmen has come round. It is a mad age. Pass the Cutty Sark, Harry. *(BAKER just stares ahead.)* Harry? *(Pause.)* You are hogging the liquor Harry!

BAKER.   Sorry, I'm a bit lost . . .

CAMBERLEY.   Wonderful. There is a crippling strike. There is an imminent take-over by communists and the minister for — what — what are you minister for Harry?

BAKER.   Get stuffed!

CAMBERLEY.   The Industry minister admits he's lost. There is an argument for Fricker in itself.

SATCHLEY.   I think the debate is deteriorating, isn't it.

PINCER.   Hear, hear.

BAKER.   Yes.

CAMBERLEY.   You say it is deteriorating. I hear no one very positive for Hacker or for Bissell. No one is arguing for them.

SATCHLEY.   I am prepared to speak for Keith —

CAMBERLEY.   Listen to the enthusiasm! She is prepared to speak! She will speak if she has to! What are the arguments for Keith? He is your protegé!

SATCHLEY.   Not at all.

CAMBERLEY.   The argument for Keith is that he will not sling us out of office. That is the extent of the argument for Keith.

SATCHLEY.   Look, do you intend to let anybody else here speak or not?

PINCER.   Hear, hear!

CAMBERLEY.   Listen, Elizabeth, I would rather hear you snivelling from the back benches than see England red as butcher's meat, and that's a fact.

DOGGITT.   You are a bit of a storm trooper, aren't you Boyd?

CAMBERLEY.   Look, Norris, either you are for the system or you are not. I am for it. And I say don't run away, put on your boots. For boots read Fricker.

SATCHLEY.   Can I make one more effort to raise the level of debate?

BAKER.   Christ, Elizabeth, sometimes I could throw up at the sound of your voice!

DOGGITT.   Oh, do shut up, Harry.

PINCER.   That is about the least constructive remark we've heard.

BAKER.   I cannot stick the sound of —

PINCER.   That really doesn't matter!

BAKER.   I am just saying —

PINCER.   Does it!

BAKER *(shrugs)*.   All right.

SATCHLEY.   I put it to you, Harry notwithstanding, the choice is between Keith and Lionel —

CAMBERLEY.   Lionel who?

SATCHLEY.   Keith and Lionel. Now, I put it to you, Keith is the more experienced, while Lionel is —

CAMBERLEY.   Lionel who?

DOGGITT.   You are not helping, Boyd!

SATCHLEY.   Lionel is popular with the police. They like him.

PINCER.   He got a standing ovation at the Hendon passing out parade.

SATCHLEY.   He has their ear.

CAMBERLEY.   Who wants their ears? What use is anybody's ear? You cannot disperse a riot with an ear. Ezra Fricker has their right arms. They will clobber joyously for him.

DOGGITT.   I move we ask Boyd belt up for ten minutes.

PINCER.   Seconded.

CAMBERLEY.   All right. Dither. Dither away.

SATCHLEY.   Lionel is also twenty yards from here.

DOGGITT.   Yes.

SATCHLEY.   He can give an instant press.

DOGGITT.   I happen to know Lionel has his speech written.

BAKER.   Everybody's speech is written. My speech is written! We are not going for a man because his speech is written!

CAMBERLEY.   May I come in?

PINCER.   No.

SATCHLEY.   He wants most of the present cabinet to remain.

BAKER.   That should sustain public confidence.

CAMBERLEY.   I suggest to you, however—

DOGGITT.   You have been —

CAMBERLEY.   I suggest to you —

DOGGITT.   Boyd —

CAMBERLEY.   Nothing will do more to wreck confidence than keeping the present incumbents in their offices. A more unpopular pack of —

DOGGITT.   Boyd!

CAMBERLEY.   A more unpopular pack of washed-out men have rarely been assembled. Thank you.

SATCHLEY.   The drawback with Lionel is that —

CAMBERLEY.   Lionel who?

SATCHLEY.   Is that he is not well-known.

CAMBERLEY *bursts out laughing. He puts his finger to his lips and makes a Shh!*

BAKER.   Elizabeth, that is the most grotesque understatement of modern time.

SATCHLEY.   All right.

DOGGITT.   He is obscure. He is obscure.

PINCER.   The country will not rally round for Lionel.

CAMBERLEY.   Lionel who?

BAKER.   His name is scarcely known outside this room.

CAMBERLEY.   And Ezra Fricker's is on every piss-shed wall!

BAKER.   I go with Boyd some of the way. I go with Boyd as far as this. If it comes to chucking Westminster —

DOGGITT.   Oh!

PINCER.   Not this again.

BAKER.   If it comes to chucking Westminster, Ezra Fricker is the man. Because if there is one thing people think of when they think of Ezra Fricker it is parliament. He is a loud boy, but he is constitutionalist. And if it needs some trimming, they will let him do it.

CAMBERLEY.   Oh, how Harry thinks! Liquor or no liquor, how he thinks.

BAKER.   When it comes to sweeping out the constitution, no one will do it better. There will be tears as big as diamonds down his cheeks.

CAMBERLEY.   Harry, I love you. But put it plainer. People like Brian could just miss the point.

BAKER.   Fricker is the perfect undertaker. That's my point.

CAMBERLEY.   When you want to do a murder, ask a policeman. That's Harry's point. *(Long pause.)*

DOGGITT.   I will tell you why Ezra Fricker will not do. *(Pause.)* It is very simple why he will not do. And it is nothing to do with parliament and constitution. We have all the powers that we want. He will not do because money doesn't want him. Money has grown too big for England. You cannot dress her in a union jack. Her arse would hang out. *(He looks round the table.)* Find what money wants, and want it. *(Pause. Sound of a crowd.)*

SATCHLEY.   All those for Lionel? *(SATCHLEY, DOGGITT & PINCER raise their hands.)* Will you ask them to let us out, please?

PINCER.   **Let us out please.** *(There is no response.)* **Let us out please!** *(Sound of chanting.)*

BAKER.   Listen. They are chanting his name out there.

Enter CARETAKER. SATCHLEY, DOGGITT, PINCER & CARE-TAKER *exit.* CAMBERLEY *and* BAKER *remain slumped in the arm-chairs with bottles. Only the clock is audible. Pause.*

BAKER.   You did well. *(Long pause. He swallows his drink.)* You did well. *(Pause.)*

CAMBERLEY.   Lionel who?

BAKER.   Quite.

CAMBERLEY.   Lionel who? *(They both drink. The* CARETAKER *re-enters with an armful of sheets.)*

SERVANT.   Gents, I must lock up.

BAKER.   We must lock up.

CAMBERLEY.   The man says.

BAKER.   What's your name?

SERVANT.   Bob.

BAKER.   Well, Bob, we have crowned the king.

SERVANT.   Yes, sir.

BAKER.   Doncha want to know who it is?

SERVANT.   I can wait for the papers, Mr Baker.

BAKER.   You can, of course.

CAMBERLEY.   Ask us. Ask us who it is.

SERVANT.   I'm sorry, I must turn you out, gents.

CAMBERLEY.   He doesn't want to know who it is! *(He turns to* BAKER.*)* He does not want to know who it is.

SERVANT *(Spreading them on the table).*   Now, if you don't clear out I will have the dust sheets over you.
CAMBERLEY.   I call that — I call that —
SERVANT.   Now come on, gents!
CAMBERLEY.   Here is a man, a servant of the House, has locked the cabinet up in a room —
BAKER.   And let 'em out again —
CAMBERLEY.   And let 'em out again, and does not give a pig's fart who they have nominated for the highest office in the land — I call that —
BAKER *(To* SERVANT*).*   Bob — Robert —
CAMBERLEY.   I call that about the lowest depth of — intellectual barrenness — I have encountered in my —
BAKER.   Bob, listen, Bob —
SERVANT.   Come on now, out!
CAMBERLEY.   In what? In fifty years of parliamentary —
BAKER.   You see, Bob, what we have here is —
CAMBERLEY.   Don't talk to him.
BAKER.   I am telling him —
CAMBERLEY.   Don't talk to him.
BAKER.   I am telling Robert what democracy is all about.
SERVANT *(Looking at his watch).*   Right. Twenty seconds.
BAKER.   Robert, I don't think even with my eloquence I could encapsulate democracy in so short a —
CAMBERLEY.   Pig ignorant.
BAKER.   Into a defintion of such pith and brevity —
CAMBERLEY.   Pig ignorance.
SERVANT.   Right. **Out.** *(To* BAKER'S *horror, he is jerked from his seat.)*
BAKER.   Good God.
SERVANT.   Come on, Sir! **Out.**
CAMBERLEY *(Draining his glass).*   Goodbye, Harry! *(As the* SERVANT *returns, he gets up.)* I think you think your time has come.
SERVANT.   The rule says the room must be emptied and locked, Mr. Camberley.
CAMBERLEY.   No. You think your time has come . . .

He walks out.

Scene ·Six

The grounds of St. Clare's mental hospital, bedecked for a fete. WIPER, *a patient, indulges a talent for impersonation. A friend,* SLAPP, *watches critically.*

WIPER *(in the style of* FRICKER*).*   I say to you — I say to you — *(He intones with deliberation.)* I say to you — there is — a horror —
SLAPP.   An horror.
WIPER.   An horror? *(Pause.)* An horror?
SLAPP.   One of his peccadilloes, is it not? *(Pause.* WIPER *prepares.)*

WIPER.   I say to you — there is an horror in my heart — there is a cold and
clammy shiver — which clamps upon my spine. I look about me — I look
about me — and I see — oh, horror! I see you feel it too! You feel — oh, yes, I
see it — you feel like me — we cannot trust our neighbour any more! Our
neighbour, upon whose arm we have been wont to rely, this same neighbour,
may he not be — horrible to say it — may he not be — my enemy? *(He points.
He leans forward.)* But I say— I say to you — are we to let the envy and the
malice of a few — the treachery of a handful — split our people up? Shall we
permit these individuals, stalking malevolently in the dark — shall we permit
them — holding as they do to a credo and an ideology totally alien to the
traditions of our race — shall we permit the sowing of dissension and
suspicion in the garden of our land — shall we be split asunder by the agents
of the Kremlin — because — because — *(He seems to select a heckler.)* Yes —
yes — it does sound — it does sound horribly familiar — yes — because —
because — the truth often is familiar, is it not? It is a habit of the truth — to be
familiar — yes — oh, yes — it is not fashionable, is it? It wears — like me — it
wears old clothes — it goes about in — it — *(He falters.)* It — *(Angrily he
tosses his hat on the ground.)* **fuck.**

He senses he is being watched. He looks round. A doctor, MALLOW *is watching.*

DR MALLOW.   What are you doing with your neck, Wiper? You will put a
knot in it.
WIPER.   Fuck. Fuck.
DR MALLOW.   Billy, I am in receipt of salary to stop the likes of you doing
self-injury.
SLAPP.   He's perfecting one of his characters.
DR MALLOW.   The Hanged Man, I suppose? Wiper I utter one word only. I
whisper it, in case you testify that I am needle-happy. *(He leans closer.)* Se —
da — tion *(Pause. He freezes in his position.)* Now will you stop?
WIPER *(relaxing).*   Bugger it.

SLAPP *and* WIPER *start to leave.*

DR MALLOW.   Mr Fricker is reading from St Paul to the Ephesians.
WIPER.   I'm not au fait with the Saint's letters, I'm afraid.
DR MALLOW.   St Paul says, 'I am coming. Get your bowls out. Be prepared
to wash my feet.'
WIPER.   Ah.
DR MALLOW.   St Paul was not cramped with humility. Not crippled with
humility like Christ. No more is Ezra Fricker.
WIPER.   No.
DR MALLOW.   Fricker expects to be called away at any minute. It is possible
he may not even get here, but will turn back at the gates, or break all
regulations and do a U-turn on the motorway. I think we must accept the
opening of hospital fetes ranks low on Mr Fricker's order of priorities. Sir
George plans an afternoon of recorded music should he be summoned to the
palace. Martial music. The hospital is to shudder to the echo of trombones
like a banana republic on the morning of a coup.
SLAPP.   You sound a shade less than enthusiastic, Dr Mallow, dare I say?

MALLOW. Me? I hope my dead doctor's drawl never suggested it. I am a houseman. We are bred to nod. *(He smiles, strolls away.)*

FRICKER'S AIDES *appear at the table.*

TUESDAY *(to* IMBER*).* Have we tested both these phones?

IMBER. Yes.

TUESDAY. And they are separate lines?

IMBER. Of course they are.

TUESDAY. They will ring bang in the middle.

IMBER. This is what we hope. He will go on reading St Paul until they do.

TUESDAY. Ah . . .

IMBER. The BBC are here. Imagine it.

TUESDAY. Quite.

IMBER. I will go to him. I will touch him on the left shoulder. He will turn, I will whisper, away from the mike, it's for you.

TUESDAY. It's for you.

IMBER. He will go to the phone. They will give him power. And the cameras will be turning. It will be pure history.

Applause. Enter FLEMING, FRICKER & DORIS.

FLEMING *(tapping the microphone).* Is this on? *(He looks around vaguely.)* Is it? *(He booms into it.)* Hello. *(It echoes around.)* Oh, yes. *(He taps it again.)* I don't think it is on, is it? Not now, is it? *(His voice echoing over the speakers.)* Apparently it is. I am told it is.

IMBER *(leaning over to him).* It most definitely is.

FLEMING. It is. *(He smiles, coughs.)* Good afternoon, ladies and gentlemen. I am Sir George Fleming, and I welcome you most heartily to the annual summer fete at St. Clare's. Today is a very special day, not only because it is our fête — our **fête** — but because, dare I say — it is the day our nation's fate — F.A.T.E. — fate is decided.

FRICKER *(leaning to* TUESDAY*).* He has taken my pun and buggered it.

FLEMING. I think I may say, with perfect modesty, the eyes of the world are upon us, or at least — *(He turns to* FRICKER.*)* on one of us, one whom I hope will not, in the clamour of high office, ever forget an afternoon —

FRICKER *(to* TUESDAY*).* My syntax is catching, is it not? Clamour of high office is very Ezra, isn't it? I have my epigones. I have become a source for after-dinner speakers.

FLEMING. An afternoon spent in the company of the less fortunate, but I think I may assure the honourable gentlemen, no less patriotic inmates of this place. *(Pause.)* It is now my pleasure, and my duty, as our nation stands at the cross-roads of its fate — To welcome on your behalf, the Right Honourable Ezra Fricker, MP.

He turns with a gesture. FRICKER *deliberately allows the applause to rise before standing and moving to the microphone. He waits for perfect silence.*

FRICKER. When there is sickness in the body, send for the physician. *(Applause. He waits.)* Lo, the physician comes! *(More applause. He lets it die.)* I was going to make a speech. *(Pause.)* Then I thought, no, there are strawberries and cream in that tent. *(Pause.)* Only a fool competes with strawberries. *(Pause.)* There are some gentlemen — and a lady — somewhere in the great city of London, attempting at this very moment to make up their minds on some — trifling matter — *(Laughter.)* but one in which I will admit I have a passing, casual interest — *(Laughter.)* and it is with them in mind that I read to you this afternoon — *(He points.)* Ah! You thought you'd get away with it! No, no, I am too much in love with my own voice — the strawberries will have to wait — *(He smiles.)* That I read to you this afternoon, St Paul. St Paul, who was not averse to shouting out advice, even though it fell on stony ground. St Paul who was a rebel by virtue of keeping faith with his ideas — and indeed, the ideas of his party! St Paul who was permanently out of date. St Paul who would not be silent, and wandered as an outcast, year in, year out. I read to you, *(He picks up a Bible.)* Corinthians, Chapter 12. 'For I fear lest when I come I shall not find you such as I would, and that I shall be found unto you such as you would not; lest there be debates, envyings, wraths, strifes, backbitings.' *(He stares at the telephones on the desk, willing them to ring.)*

WIPER *(watching from the crowd).*   He sweats. I never knew. He sweats.

SLAPP.   He is human.

WIPER.   But sweat? When I feel him most, when I am absolutely him, on a perfect day, it never occurs to me to sweat . . .

SLAPP.   It's hot up there.

WIPER.   No. Our skin is not like that. The moisture is something else. I think we are in pain.

DR MALLOW *(appearing behind them).*   Are you the duckling scoop?

SLAPP.   Beg pardon?

DR MALLOW.   Are you in charge of the scoop-a-duckling stall?

SLAPP.   Yes, sir.

DR MALLOW.   Then would you be so kind as to stand by? The Right Honourable will eventually run out of St Paul. Then he will want to spend some coppers, I expect. *(They go out. FRICKER, in desperation, is near the end of his recital.)*

FRICKER.   'The night is far spent, the day is at hand! Let us therefore cast off the works of darkness, and let us put on the armour of light!' *(Pause. The telephone has not rung. FRICKER looks to his AIDES.)* It has not rung. *(Some directions are being issued over the speaker. DORIS looks at FRICKER, her hands folded in her lap.)* It has not rung.

IMBER.   No.

FRICKER.   I gave it an abundance of opportunity. I created moments for that telephone an actor would have envied.

IMBER.   Never mind.

FRICKER.   Never mind. Never mind, he says.

IMBER.   Well, what can I —

FRICKER.   Quite. It never was a palliative to say never mind.

IMBER.   No.

FRICKER.   It is as useless as a sticking plaster on a disembowelling.

IMBER.   I apologize.

FRICKER *(to* TUESDAY *).*   Are the cameras with us?

TUESDAY.   Following like beggars.

FRICKER.   We will do the walkabout.

TUESDAY.   I wonder if we shouldn't go to London.

FRICKER. Dick, I solemnly advise you not to make persistent reference to that place. I do, most solemnly. *(He turns to DORIS.)* My dear? *(She gets up, slowly.)* Stay by me, please. Be my dog.

IMBER. I am ringing Harry.

FRICKER. As you wish. *(IMBER slips away. FLEMING appears.)*

FLEMING. This is St. Clare's weather.

FRICKER. Is it?

FLEMING. St Clare's weather always ends up in a storm.

FRICKER. How very appropriate. What you might describe as a nosh-up followed by a wash-out!

Laughter, sycophantic and otherwise, as they move away into the fête. Behind FRICKER and his AIDES, FLEMING and DORIS.

FLEMING. I always think of the wives at times like this. I ask myself what goes on in the minds of the wives.

DORIS. Usually they wet themselves.

FLEMING. What?

DORIS. Foul their underwear.

FLEMING. Look, Ezra has won a goldfish!

DORIS. Are you a doctor?

FLEMING. I an a neurosurgical psychiatrist.

DORIS. Yes, but are you a doctor?

FLEMING. A sort of doctor, a specialist.

DORIS. Good. I need a doctor.

FLEMING. Really?

DORIS. I think I may be going mad.

FLEMING. We all get that feeling now and again.

DORIS. I wish you wouldn't walk away. When I am talking to you.

FLEMING. I am keeping up with Mr Fricker, Mrs Fricker.

DORIS. Help me, will you?

FLEMING. I think the camera's on us. Yes, it is.

DORIS *(stopping)*. **Will you help me!**

FLEMING. Oh, look, a coconut shy!

DORIS. I was under the impression that you swore an oath.

FLEMING. Yes.

DORIS. To help the sick.

FLEMING. Yes.

DORIS. Right. Stick to it.

FLEMING. All right.

DORIS. Thank you.

FLEMING *(tossing a ball wildly)*. Oh, dear!

DORIS. I would like to see my husband dead.

FLEMING. Does he know that?

DORIS. No, of course not.

FLEMING. It is a relatively common aspiration, I believe.

DORIS. The trouble is, I mean it.

FLEMING. Look, Ezra's won a goldfish.

DORIS. Look in my bag.

FLEMING. Must keep up. I think.

DORIS.   Look in my bag, I said. *(She holds it open to him. There is a pistol inside.)*

FRICKER *(as* IMBER *sidles up to him).*   What's happening? I cannot sustain enthusiasm for these endless games of quoits. I have a box of allsorts in one hand and a goldfish in the other. I shall run out of hands.

IMBER.   They are still in session.

FRICKER.   Still in session?

IMBER.   Harry says.

FRICKER.   That is a bad omen.

IMBER.   I don't see that.

FRICKER.   It is a terrible omen. It is a terrible omen when the true and proper candidate stays unannounced.

IMBER.   Not at all.

FRICKER.   They are conspiring against me.

IMBER.   Not necessarily.

FRICKER.   They are conspiring to thwart the popular will! *(He turns to the* STALLHOLDER *holding up a dart.)* Now, what am I supposed to do with this? Pierce the Ace of Spades? Well, I am nothing if not a contemner of the fates. Have I not flown in the face of what our lords and masters call inevitable? It is only fitting I should pierce the ace, I, who believe nothing to be inevitable, I should stab it, should I not? And what is my reward for this? *(The man mutters.)* A quid? A quid for murdering my fate? My friend says a quid. I am not sure he is keeping pace with inflation, but then, who is? Clearly it is the going rate for fate-killers, it is the rate for the skill. Now, there is a lesson in economics! Dart-players cannot command the rates they have done hitherto. Now, is that because there is a surplus of darts players, or a fall in demand? The laws of economics, you see, operate even at the fairground stall.

IMBER.   He is steaming. He is wonderful to watch . . .

TUESDAY.   He wouldn't hear the phone ring if it did.

IMBER.   And it won't do. It won't ring now, will it?

FRICKER *(throws a dart).*   Missed. Well, I shall negotiate a second chance. Fifteen pence? *(Mutter from* STALLHOLDER, *and laughter from public.)* Why should I not negotiate? There is no statutory price control, is there?

TUESDAY.   The TV crew are packing up. They are winding up their cables.

FRICKER *(playing to crowd and media).*   But the gentleman accepts my offer! It is a free market, is it not? Am I not entitled to make my bid, untrammelled by the stranglehold of legislation? Yes, I am, and the result is that the price has dropped! I am nothing if not loyal to my own ideas!

IMBER.   Suggest he moves on, will you? He is getting wild about the eyes.

TUESDAY.   Yes.

IMBER.   Nudge him, then.

FRICKER.   Third time! Third time lucky!

TUESDAY.   There is a duck stall over there . . .

FRICKER *(to* STALLHOLDER*).*   Ten pence! Ten pence! What do you say to ten? *(The man shrugs with embarrassment.)* You accept it? *(He shrugs.)* He accepts it! Robbery? Do I hear robbery? There is no such thing as robbery in business, there is only the price agreed. The man is exercising his right to accept a lower price. I am an advert for good housekeeping, am I not? I am a living advertisement for the free market, and is it not a most beneficial institution? I am buying my dart at one half of the original cost! *(He throws it. It misses again.)* I must try again!

IMBER. Ezra —

FRICKER. Obviously I must try again!

IMBER. Ezra —

FRICKER. No, I am not defeated yet! As long as I have money in my pocket, I am not defeated yet!

IMBER. Come on, Ezra, they are going cold.

FRICKER *(turning on him).* Stop trying to usher me! I will not be ushered. I have not triumphed yet. A dart! Sell me a dart.

STALLHOLDER. Thirty.

FRICKER. Thirty? Thirty?

STALLHOLDER. Thirty.

FRICKER. It was ten pence just now. *(The man shrugs.)* A rise of three hundred per cent in the blink of an eyelid. *(He shrugs again.)* I see. I see the gentleman can read the signs. He sees the market for darts is picking up. Obviously I must pay or quit.

IMBER. Quit.

FRICKER. Quit, he says! A voice says quit! But I am no quitter.

STALLHOLDER. Forty.

FRICKER. Forty? Forty now? The market is in earnest! *(A clap of thunder.)* Even the gods are moved to speak! But to what purpose? It is always a problem with the gods, their signs are open to a variety of interpretations! *(It begins to rain. People move away.)*

IMBER. Call it a day. Come on, call it a day.

FRICKER. I have only twenty pence! Will someone lend me twenty pence? I have no change! *(Finding himself alone.)* And they all wanted me. In alleys and hovels they wanted me . . .

Enter SLAPP *and* WIPER

SLAPP. Mr Fricker . . . *(*FRICKER *looks, with amazement, at* WIPER *who adopts a waxworks pose, freezing in a gesture reminiscent of Fricker himself.* FRICKER *wanders over.)* He used to be Napoleon. But there are so many Napoleons here.

WIPER *(as* FRICKER *gazes at him).* The citadel is under siege! The enemy is at the gates! The fortress shudders with the convulsion of its fate! I say to the inhabitants, look to your backs, beware the alien within! *(He stops, freezes.)*

FRICKER. Good. Very good.

WIPER. I have a fear. A terrible fear, which gnaws and fixes on my soul. I am haunted by the spectre of civil war. I see master against man, and man against master, I see wife against husband, and father against son! *(He stops. Pause.)*

FRICKER. You do me very well. *(He starts to go away.)*

WIPER. One more. *(*FRICKER *stops.)* Do not leave me on my own. Do not leave me on my own. Do not leave me on my own . . . *(Pause. he looks up and smiles.)*

FRICKER. Now, that one I don't think is really me. But the others, yes, you do have a knack, don't you?

Enter DR MALLOW.

MALLOW.   Billy, are you pestering the gentleman? Run along and queue for
   tea. *(The patients leave.)*
FRICKER.   You are a doctor?
MALLOW.   A low houseman.
FRICKER.   As a low houseman, will you give me a short definition of
   insanity?
MALLOW.   Preferring love to sex. Grass to concrete. Working to dole.
FRICKER.   You are a cynic, I see.
MALLOW.   Not in the least. Nothing is more likely to bring depression than
   adherence to a defunct idea.
FRICKER.   And if the idea should be a right one?
MALLOW.   Now you are invoking non-scientific criteria. I am a houseman,
   not a moralist. *(Leaves.)*

Enter TUESDAY & IMBER.

FRICKER.   Where's Doris?
TUESDAY.   With Sir George.
IMBER.   I rather doubt you want to know this but it's Bissell. Bissell is the one
   they went for. *(Pause.)* Did you want to know it? *(Pause.)* No, I didn't think
   you did.
FRICKER.   Nigel, the identity of the particular drone who is no doubt at the
   moment winging his way towards the queen bee's nest, is, frankly, a matter of
   supreme indifference to me.
IMBER.   Yes, of course.
FRICKER.   Why should I care which of these aspirants to a footnote has
   achieved success?
IMBER.   I can't think.
FRICKER.   There is, I assure you, no significance whatsoever in his having
   succeeded. There is only significance in my having failed.
IMBER.   Quite. He was greeted with boos. The stock market has gone down
   fifty points. They say Victoria Street is ankle deep in glass. I personally don't
   think this is the end of it.
FRICKER.   You personally don't think so.
IMBER.   No.
FRICKER.   Well, what about that? Nigel Imber does not think this is the end
   of it. I can only agree with him. The end of what, though?
IMBER.   Ezra Fricker.
TUESDAY.   I am all for democracy —
FRICKER.   You are an MP!
TUESDAY.   Yes, and I am all for democracy, but I say, get in the car, go back
   to London, and lead the mob.
FRICKER.   Well, what are MPs coming to?
TUESDAY.   I am only saying I —
FRICKER.   Do not think that idea has been staggering against the ropes of my
   imagination these last fifteen years? Do you not think I knew from my first
   utterance I could bring the monster back onto the streets? That I could send
   the pavements flying and lay the buses flat? I did. Of course I did. I knew I

could bring them back, and all parliament knew it too. Why else was I the pariah of pariahs? But I will tell you where it leads to. To the clink.

TUESDAY.   Parliament is done for. I'm sorry, but it's done for.

FRICKER.   And I am too. I am not sure I see much glory in being carried shoulder high by lorry drivers. It is not so to speak, an element of my world picture. *(Pause.)* Wait for me in the car. You can plot your futures. No need for you to sink with me. I have no doubt there are others in whose turnups you might be carried to the top.

IMBER.   That's extremely unkind, Ezra.

FRICKER.   Yes, I am unkind. It is an unkind age we live in. You see me in the basement of my fate. There is only one floor lower.

IMBER.   Death?

FRICKER.   Oxford. I shall revert to Don and be the butt of soppy humour as I cross the quad.

FRICKER'S LONDON. ON THE TOMB OF THE UNKNOWN WARRIOR.

Fricker's Voice

The Dead. There is no patriotism without the Dead. There can be no nation without war, because blood is the price of nationhood, and without the sacrifice of blood the race cannot be born and reborn through the fountain of its broken veins. In this one war a million English died. Their bones are dust on Sinai, by the Euphrates, in Venetia, Macedon, Flanders, Picardy. Called from their homes, they flung their flesh into the fight. It is the fashion to decry war, to question and insinuate. But there the intellectual draws the blinds on his perception, for blood speaks, blood mutters unto blood . . .

Scene Seven

The Crypt of St Paul's. In a thin shaft of light, an urn on a pedestal and a vase of flowers. A woman, in mourning, stands in the fringes of the light. It is SATCH-LEY. Footsteps are heard approaching, slowly, regularly. They stop.

SATCHLEY. Norris?
DOGGITT. Yes.
SATCHLEY. Kiss me. *(He walks towards her, stops.)* Without crumpling my hat. *(He kisses her cheek.)* Loathed him.
DOGGITT. Yes.
SATCHLEY. His eye.
DOGGITT. Awful.
SATCHLEY. Staring bloody cyc.
DOGGITT. Pop.
SATCHLEY. What?
DOGGITT. The eyes.
SATCHLEY. Where?
DOGGITT. In the oven.
SATCHLEY. In the oven?
DOGGITT. Furnace.
SATCHLEY. Do they?
DOGGITT. Pop!
SATCHLEY. Pop! *(She goes to the urn, looks at it.)* The widow wanted it all modest. She was after something private. I said not on your life. I said if she tried this in some suburban crematorium or rooky churchyard I'd plaster injunctions over it. I said I'd have the body snatched pro bono publico. I was never more terrible.
DOGGITT. I can imagine.
SATCHLEY. This is the nation's treat.
DOGGITT. Quite.
SATCHLEY. Have you seen upstairs yet? The aisles are packed with specimens I thought extinct. Sad little men in shiny suits, fragrant of fish shops. Hill farmers all nicked with shaving. Shoving the Cambridge economists to get a seat. The party in her many colours. The ragamuffin patriots. When we die, Norris, will they polish the toecaps of their boots?
DOGGITT. No.
SATCHLEY. Flocking in from slum and shire. Hiring buses in dismal Midlands constituencies . . .
DOGGITT. No. I know how it will be when I die. It will be as if a sheet of paper had slid off a desk. I suppose that is him, is it? *(She stares at him.)* I mean, did anybody actually see him? Dead?
SATCHLEY. Norris.
DOGGITT. I ask because in actual fact did anybody —
SATCHLEY. Norris. *(Pause. he turns on his heel.)*
DOGGITT. Come on. Hurry up.

They go out. Pause. A figure appears out of the shadows. It is DORIS in mourning. She is drinking from a flask. She looks at the urn.

DORIS.   Going next to Lawrence of Arabia. I said you'd like that, I said — do keep still, I'm talking to you, keep bloody — *(Pause.)* Dancing to the underground . . . all of you . . . jigging in your little urns . . . last tango of the yobs of history . . . *(A figure comes in, watches from a respectable distance. It is* CRYSTAL *in mourning.)*

CRYSTAL.   Oh.

DORIS *(tucking the bottle into her handbag).*   Yes?

CRYSTAL.   Cold, isn't it? A rather chilly crypt.

DORIS.   I'm perfectly all right.

CRYSTAL.   Yes. *(Pause.)* Yes, of course. *(She turns to go.)*

DORIS.   Were you one of his mistresses?

CRYSTAL.   I'm Crystal Backlawn. President of RIPCORD.

DORIS.   RIPCORD?

CRYSTAL.   Refugees in Peril Co-ordinating Committee.

DORIS.   Ah. Not one of his favourite charities.

CRYSTAL.   No.

DORIS.   Not a very perfect Christian, all in all. Loved the vengeance, ditched the rest. Did you say you were one of his mistresses? Do say if you were, I wouldn't mind. Only I hate the way they skulk at funerals like a counter-demonstration *(Pause.)*

CRYSTAL.   He longed to lay his weary head on my proud breasts.

DORIS.   Ah.

CRYSTAL.   In Greek.

DORIS.   Of course.

CRYSTAL.   A pentameter this was. Circa 1943.

DORIS.   I know the line. Only by the time it got to me, his head was proud and my breasts were weary.

CRYSTAL.   Confusion of the case endings.

DORIS.   No. He liked to think of me as weary. As stretched and spoiled by suffering. It turned him on.

A figure has appeared from the shadows and moves towards the urn. The women look at him. He is a schoolboy. He stands staring at the urn.

NATLEY.   Shall we, who flung our nets across the skies and drew unto ourselves the homage of the firmament of nations, not know one another when we clash shoulders in the dark? *(Pause. He looks to* DORIS.*)* Bexhill. 1963.

DORIS.   Is it?

NATLEY.   The darkness is here.

DORIS.   Yes.

NATLEY.   Oh, yes . . . *(He gazes at the urn, fixedly.)*

DORIS *(to* CRYSTAL*).*   Did you find him a good lover? I mean did he — fuck — well?

CRYSTAL.   I couldn't honestly say. *(They pause, stare at him. He goes out. Pause.)*

DORIS.   I used to wonder whether it was him or me. The wandering attention, the rather stiff and heavy motion of our limbs, like turning clay with a matchstick. Or is it always like that? When I looked at him, when he was dead, I thought, oh, you dear thing, did we make the earth move, ever? I wonder if we did. *(She takes the bottle out, drinks some.)*

CRYSTAL. You are so frank.
DORIS. He loved frankness. Frankness with a bloody maw. Great man, you see. I mean that. He damned well was.
CRYSTAL. Yes.
DORIS. Oh, yes. And I should know. I washed the shit off his knickers.

A man enters, in a dark suit. He stands some way away.

STREATHAM. Mrs Fricker? Alan Streatham.
DORIS *(shoving the bottle away).* Ah.
STREATHAM. Labour party.
DORIS. Know it.
STREATHAM. Not listening to the speeches?
DORIS. No.
STREATHAM. I suppose everyone will be coming up to you today.
DORIS. Yes . . .
STREATHAM. And saying 'I remember —' That will be the phrase of the day, won't it? The introit to a thousand anecdotes? I remember, on the Common Market once, he said to me, Alan, we are the undertakers of the nation. And as a good socialist, I said, Ezra, happy are the people so delivered of their burden. He smiled at me, very thin that smile of his, the smile of superior insight doomed never to be communicated, and he said, I loved his metaphors 'People minus Nation, castration. People plus Nation, Exaltation.' And I think now he was right.
DORIS. Well, blow me down.
STREATHAM. It's good to see the House of Commons almost as a body here. All parties brought together like this. In honouring him, we show ourselves united. And Ezra never held high office. You must be very proud.
DORIS. I'm drunk.
STREATHAM. Sorry?
DORIS *(turning away).* Oh, fuck . . . *(STREATHAM looks at her, then turns away. pause.)*
CRYSTAL. I wish . . .
DORIS *(extending the bottle).* Have some of this.
CRYSTAL. What?
DORIS. Go on, have sme.
CRYSTAL *(taking a swig).* I wish — *(She hands it back.)* I wish now I had let him fondle me. Well, more than that. Do you mind this.
DORIS. Me? No, I don't mind this.
CRYSTAL. Because there's going to be this stampede now, this scraping out the bowels of memory to find the actual Ezra Fricker, isn't there? Awful nancy little dons calling at our homes and asking, with that shifting bum of tact and candour, did he lay you? And I should have to answer no, which is dull, so very dull, I think. Do you mind this?
DORIS. Me? No, I don't mind this . . .
CRYSTAL. So I thought of lying and saying yes, the once, upon this very sofa, between Hector my first and Benedict the second of my children, which puts it somewhere in the middle fifties, doesn't it? Would you mind that?
DORIS. Me? No, why should I mind that?
CRYSTAL. I do so envy you.

DORIS.   Envy me?

CRYSTAL.   Oddly. Really envy you. *(DORIS shrugs, drinks.)*

A man enters, in black

TICE.   Oh, Doris . . .

DORIS.   Please, Ralph, I am delicate . . .

TICE.   Oh, Doris . . . *(He embraces her.)*

DORIS. Do you know Crystal Backlawn?

TICE.   The king is dead.

DORIS.   Quite.

TICE.   I loved him, D.

DORIS.   Yes.

TICE.   Loved all of him.

DORIS.   Me too.

TICE.   No better wife.

DORIS.   No better friend Ralph.

TICE.   Nope. *(He shakes his head.)* Nope.

DORIS.   There . . .

TICE *(of the urn).*   Oh, look at him . . . he does look fine . . . he does . . .

DORIS.   He's going in the wall, Ralph.

TICE. They couldn't keep him out of 'ere. There 'asn't been an Englishman since Churchill better qualified to come in 'ere . . .

DORIS.   It's what he would have wanted. In fact, he kept on mentioning it. Never mind me, I said, you get in there if you can. I'll go with my mum and dad . . . *(She takes a drink.)*

TICE.   I see the bastard Norris fawning round yer. Where did 'e touch yer? Wash yer 'ands.

DORIS.   I have been kissed and fondled by representatives of every social, religious and political opinion in the land. I am a finger-printed testimony to pluralism . . . *(She turns to* CRYSTAL.*)*

TICE.   'Ere they come! They crack with starch and creak with leather but their gobs are red with sucking brains. 'Is brains!

DORIS.   Oh, God! *(She takes a last swig at the bottle.)*

TICE *(to the urn).*   Oh, son, the whimpering of the epigones . . .

The mourners arrive in the crypt. Swaying and shuffling and chanting from the third canto of Dante's Inferno. They form a circle round the urn. After a pause, NATLEY *steps forward.*

NATLEY.   An English Schoolboy's Farewell to his Hero. *(Pause.)*
Into the earth then carry him
Who bore alone the standard of his race.
In ridicule they showered him
Who pride in country he would not debase.
Now blind with tears the people shuffle
Shamed to silence, their quarrels a disgrace.
He knew, though foes beset us, we are mighty
If in God, Queen and Country we only bathe our face.

He steps back.

TICE.　Very good. He would 'ave liked that.

CRYSTAL.　Shh.

TICE.　Wouldn't 'e, Doris? Smart kid.

SATCHLEY.　There comes a time, in the retreat from principle, in the abject surrender to the current of events, in the capitulation to compromise and the expedient, when from some quarter comes the cry Stop! Thus far and no further! *(Pause.)* His was this voice, a voice unmuted by the roar of fashionable contempt, a voice which touched and stirred the very springs of national consciousness, a voice heard, and heard, heeded, echoing down the corridors of history!

SLADE.　History, oh, history, yes . . . History, she says.

EADY *(looking along the line.)* Brian?

SATCHLEY *(undeterred).*　We lay his ashes in the company of heroes, but we bear his purpose in our life.

SLADE.　Is that History trying to get in? Lock the doors, somebody, it will have its hands around our throats.

DOGGITT.　Who is it?

JEAL.　Can't see.

SLADE.　Somebody summoned it! Now it will get in! Whoever called it? It's here!

SLADE.　Draw your coats tighter round you! Tuck your trousers in your socks!

TICE.　Who in Christ's —

SLADE.　Our poor white flesh was not made for standing up to this!

SATCHLEY.　Norris.

DOGGITT.　It's —

SLADE.　Listen! Oh, listen! The grinding jaws of **judgement**! Hide your face!

JEAL.　Archie, will you — love —

NOYES.　This is a demo, isn't it?

SATCHLEY.　Norris.

DOGGITT.　I don't think anybody —

SLADE.　Me? Strip him of his garments? Rob him of his raiment and strut in another's clothes? Not me!

NOYES.　I'm fucked if I will tolerate this. We are putting a great man in the wall! Show a bit of bloody respect!

SATCHLEY.　Archie . . .

JEAL.　Shift him — Archie —

SLADE.　Oh, they come to take me! Strike off his ear!

NOYES.　Loony bugger —

SLADE *(as they drag him away).*　Silence him! But can you strangle History? *(Pause.)*

SATCHLEY *(to* DORIS *).*　I think we're ready, dear. *(Pause.)*

CRYSTAL.　Doris.

TICE.　Love *(She does not move.)*

DOGGITT.　The jar . . . *(She is still motionless.* SATCHLEY *steps forward decisively, goes to take the urn,)*

SATCHLEY.　I will.

The assembly begins to murmur from the Third Canto.

DORIS.   Don't touch it.
SATCHLEY.   He belongs to us now.

DORIS *suddenly slaps* SATCHLEY *across the face.*

DORIS.   I said don't touch it.
SATCHLEY.   That was very silly.
CRYSTAL.   She's desperately tired.
SATCHLEY.   We're all tired. But we don't go around slapping one another.
DOGGITT.   Elizabeth?
SATCHLEY.   I'm all right.
DOGGITT.   Do you want me to —
SATCHLEY.   Don't fuss.
DORIS.   Fucking woman.
NATLEY.   Oh, shame . . .!
DORIS.   I really wanted to do that.
CRYSTAL.   Yes.
DORIS.   Yes.
NATLEY.   Oh, shame . . .!
TICE.   Take it, Doris, 'e was your man . . .
CRYSTAL.   I could. If you don't want to.
DORIS.   No.
CRYSTAL.   I will. Shall I?
TICE.   'O is this woman? Doris?

DORIS *goes forward, takes the urn in her hands. The assembly begin the Third Canto again. She moves forward some paces, stops. The urn slips out of her hands, crashes to the floor. The murmuring stops, in shocked silence. Out of the silence comes a terrible moan. It is* NATLEY. *He hurries forward, falls to his knees by the scattered ashes. He stares at them some moments, then leans further and further forward until his lips are near the floor.*

TICE.   'E's eating 'em . . . *(Pause.)* Jesus Christ . . . 'e's eating 'em . . .   .

There is a sudden scurrying activity. EADY *and* JEAL *go to pull* NATLEY *off.*

JEAL.   Little beast!
DOGGITT.   Stop the press, please.
NOYES.   Anybody got a dustpan?
DOGGITT.   Shut up, Archie.
NOYES.   Well, has anybody?
DOGGITT.   Do not let the press men out . . .
SATCHLEY.   I wonder what Lawrence of Arabia thinks of this . . .
NOYES.   Not just leaving 'em there, are we? Norris? Elizabeth?
DOGGITT.   There will be a statement later.
NOYES.   Are we?
SATCHLEY.   Yes.

With an inspiration, she goes to the vase, removes a single flower and drops it on the ashes. Relieved by her gesture, the embarrassed mourners follow suit, leaving one by one. Reprise of Handel's 'Why Do The Nations?' and fade to black.

Birth on a Hard Shoulder

'Birth on a Hard Shoulder' was first performed at the Royal Dramatic Theatre, Stockholm on 8 November 1980.

The cast were:

ERICA	Gunilla Olsson
HILARY	Marika Lindström
FINNEY	Ingvar Hirdwall
BRILLIANT	Rolf Adolfsson
CROYDON	Bengt Brunskog
FLUX	Björn Gustafson
SPECTRE	Nils Eklund
RUTKIN	Sture Hovstadius
METHS	Bo Lindström
NATTRESS	Georg Arlin
GLORIA	Gerthi Kulle
JACKIE	Monica Edwardsson
HAMMICK	Gudmar Wivesson
FIRST BEEFEATER ⎫	
SECOND BEEFEATER ⎬	omitted in this production
OFFICER OF GUARD ⎭	
FIRST PRIVATE	Björn Strand
SECOND PRIVATE	Gudmar Wivesson
TWO OTHERS	omitted
STATIONMAN	Göte Grefbo
WARDER	Björn Strand
THREE INMATES	Juan Casanova, Lennart Forss, Tommy Ringart

Directed by Barbro Larsson
Designed by Lars-Ake Thessman.

ACT ONE

Scene One

A telephone is ringing. Dim lights on a motorway emergency phone. A girl rushes on, turns, bawls to someone off.

ERICA.   Stay there! Stay in the bleedin' car, you fool! *(She picks up the receiver.)*

TELEPHONE.   Dish of the Day presents Shepherd's Vegetable —

ERICA *(slamming it down again).*   Fuck. *(Pause.)* Fuck. *(She closes her eyes for some seconds, turns and shouts.)* They're all the same! *(Pause. She picks it up again.)*

TELEPHONE.   Half a shoulder of home produced lamb — *(She replaces the receiver, waits. Then stealthily advances on it, whipping it off the hook.)*

ERICA *(yelling.)*   It's a Morris Minor — it's grey — I got the bonnet up but steam kept —

TELEPHONE.   Seventy-five grammes or three onces of dripping — half a kilo or one pound of brussel sprouts —

ERICA.   It started bumping — you know — it went a bit and then — it stopped and —

TELEPHONE.   Fifty grammes or two ounces of demerara sugar —

ERICA **My mate's having a baby! Help!** *(She grits her teeth. Pause.)*

TELEPHONE.   Score the lamb skin — rub in a little seasoning — place in a roasting tin with dripping — roast at 400 degrees or gas mark 6 — for one hour — or until well cooked —

As she stands by the phone, defeated and resigned, HILARY *comes on. She is in the advanced stage of labour. She holds her belly, screws up her face*

HILARY.   You're going to have to do it, Erica . . .

ERICA.   Never a bloody copper when you want one . . .

TELEPHONE.   Boil the sprouts slightly — drain — add butter and sugar —

ERICA.   Where's all the traffic gone? Like the end of the world here. On a bloody motorway. **Where's it gone!**

TELEPHONE.   Cook gently — serve with roast potatoes — and brown gravy —

HILARY.   Watching the election, I expect . . .

TELEPHONE.   Ring this number again tomorrow for Budget Bingo — an economy dish for Thursday.

ERICA.   Whatever comes along, I'll lie in front of it —

HILARY *(wincing.)* **Oh, shit!**
ERICA *(running her hands through her hair).* Oh, fuck . . .
TELEPHONE. Dish of the Day presents — Shepherd's Veg —

ERICA rips the receiver loose, drops it.

HILARY *(in pain).* **Shit . . .! Shit . . .!** *(She sits down on the verge.)*
ERICA. You should have gone to classes. I wish you had gone to classes, Hilary. Why didn't you go? It wouldn't have hurt you to go, would it? I don't think it's a compromise, I think it's fucking sensible, I think — **There's a car!**

Headlights from off right. ERICA hurtles into the fast lane. There is a sound of extreme braking. The lights become stationary.

Well, get out, then, you daft sod! **Get out!**

Sound of hands beating on the body panels of a Jaguar. ERICA reappears.

He won't get out! He thinks I'm gonna mug him and he won't get out! *(Sound of engine revving.)* Bloody hell, he's going!

The headlight beams travel slowly over HILARY, lying on her back, and stop.

No, he's not! He's not! He's gettin' out! *(A door slams. ERICA giggles with relief, stops.)* Wha's the matter with him?

FINNEY appears. There is blood all over his shirt, which is open at the neck. ERICA looks at him.

I'm sorry . . . I just . . . my mate's having a . . . you better go . . . sorry . . . *(He just stares at HILARY.)* **Look, fuck off will you!**
FINNEY. She should be on her side.
ERICA. Who are you?
FINNEY. I've been at two births and they —
ERICA. **Who are you?**
FINNEY. Finney. I am a stockbroker.
HILARY. The book says you — stop him gawping at me — I can't bear to be
FINNEY. Sorry —
HILARY. **Who's got the book!** *(ERICA runs off.)* Christ . . .!
FINNEY. At the hospital where I — where we — they seemed to go for the — I think it's called a lateral position —
HILARY. **Shut up!**
ERICA *(hurrying on, thumbing through the pages).* Curative values of the afterbirth — no pain with herbs — the mind at one with nature —
HILARY. **It's coming out!**
ERICA *(dropping the book).* Will you —
FINNEY. Shall I —
HILARY. Oh, God . . .!
FINNEY *(kneeling by HILARY'S knees).* I've only witnessed this — I haven't —
HILARY. Christ . . . Christ . . .!
ERICA. Haven't had a baby?
FINNEY. Not myself.

ERICA. Oh, dear.

FINNEY. Can't take responsibility for what —

ERICA. Get on with it!

FINNEY. God, it's —

HILARY. It's out. I can feel it. Is it out? *(Pause. FINNEY is looking at the child.)* Why was it so easy. Is it out?

ERICA. Easier than a crap, darling.

HILARY. You cut the cord. The long thing. Cut it.*(Pause.)* Shall I do it? *(FINNEY shakes his head.)* Then you knot it. Near its stomach. *(FINNEY gets up and goes away.)* Where's he going? *(She turns to ERICA)* Erica, look at it. **Look at it please.** *(ERICA scrambles up, goes to see. Pause.)*

ERICA. What do I do with it?

HILARY. It's dead.

ERICA. What shall I do with it?

HILARY. It's dead.

ERICA. I'll hold it upside down. Clear the mucus out of its gob. Shall I shake it? **Mister, is it dead?**

FINNEY *(turning)* It's a Labour government. They have put back a Labour government.

ERICA . **The ba-by!** *(Pause.)*

HILARY. I knew it was dead. When they slide out like that. It means they're dead.

ERICA. We don't know yet —

HILARY. **Read the book!** *(Pause. She sits up on her elbows. Sees FINNEY and the bloodstain on his shirt.)* Is that my blood? *(She turns to ERICA.)* Blimey, is that my blood?

FINNEY. Lucky. Lucky not to see this. Decided not to, obviously. Still-born baby says no to socialism. Do you see?

ERICA. Belt up.

FINNEY. First new baby under socialism kills itself.

ERICA. **Will you fucking well belt up!** *(Pause. FINNEY stares at them a moment.)*

FINNEY. I have just killed my family. *(Pause. They stare at him and his shirt.)*

ERICA. Ah.

HILARY. What? **What did he say?**

FINNEY. Got to. If you care. Only decent thing a man can do.

HILARY. **What did he say!**

ERICA. Nothing.

HILARY. He did — he said —

ERICA. All right, darling —

HILARY. **Jesus Christ.**

ERICA. **Shut up!** *(Pause.)* We've got to — someone's got to cut this cord thing — you wouldn't have — **Don't just stand there, do something!**

Blackout.

Scene Two

A room in a police headquarters. Two small tables. A coat-stand with three overcoats. On the first table, three peaked caps. At the other, three high-ranking officers sit round a ouija board. The only sound is that of the tumbler revolving under their fingers. A patient pause.

BRILLIANT. Would the spirit identify itself? *(The glass goes on.)* Please? *(and on)* Have you got a name? *(and on)* No? A number, then? Or symbol? *(and on)* Well, have you got a message, then? *(It races.)* Is the spirit angry with us? Have we offended you?

CROYDON. Does it talk English?

BRILLIANT. What?

CROYDON. English. Does it speak English. Ask it.

BRILLIANT. Do you speak English? *(The glass stops at the word 'NO'.)*

CROYDON. Thought so. Is the message for me? Ask it.

BRILLIANT. Is the message for Don? *(The glass flies to 'YES'.)* Yes, it is for Don. *(It starts racing round again.)* Would you care to spell it out for him?

CROYDON. Not English, is it?

BRILLIANT. No, but —

CROYDON. Can't then, can it?

BRILLIANT. Well, what am I supposed to —

CROYDON. Would it prefer oriental characters. Ask it.

BRILLIANT. We haven't got any oriental —

CROYDON. Ask it. Just ask it.

BRILLIANT. Would you prefer to write in oriental characters? *(The glass flies to 'YES'.)* It would. So where does that —

CROYDON. Wait.

BRILLIANT. End of dialogue.

CROYDON. Just wait! *(Long pause.)* Ask it — can we employ Direct Transcription.

BRILLIANT. Can we employ Direct Transcription? Please? *(The glass goes to 'YES'.)* Apparently.

CROYDON. Through the Alternate Digital Sphere?

BRILLIANT. Through what?

CROYDON. The Al-ter-nate Dig-i-tal Sphere.

BRILLIANT. Through the Alternate Digital Sphere? *(The glass goes to 'YES'.)* Yes.

CROYDON. Right. When I say 'NOW' take your fingers off the glass. When I say 'NOW' a second time, replace it by the same finger of the left hand. Ready? **Now.** *(They all lift off their fingers.)* **Now.** *(They change hands. Pause.)* Is it still with us?

BRILLIANT. Gone dead.

CROYDON. Ask it. You haven't asked it.

BRILLIANT. Sorry. Are you still with us? *(The glass goes to 'YES'.)* Yes he is.

CROYDON. Now it can write in English, see? Ask for a message.

BRILLIANT. Have you got your message now? For Don. *(The glass rushes off to the letters.)* Christ! *(He begins reading off the words.)* Hell-o Ser-geant Prett-y Boy —

FLUX. **Jesus ...**

CROYDON. It's my old houseboy. From Malaya. Hello, Suzie, how's Malaya? *(He grins with pleasure.)* Ask him. How's Malaya?

BRILLIANT. How's Malaya, Suzie. Don says. *(The glass moves round.)* No — fun — with — out — you — lover —

FLUX. **Christ Almighty ...**

BRILLIANT *(reading out).* Not sex-y.

CROYDON *(grinning).* Oh, why not? Ask him.

BRILLIANT. Why not? Don says. *(The glass travels.)* Mass-age my butt-ocks.

FLUX. **Jesus ...**

CROYDON *(luxuriating).* Any time, tell him. Any time.

BRILLIANT *(reading).* Kiss — my — kiss — my —

CROYDON. Come on!

BRILLIANT. Kiss my — getting stuck — kiss — my — nope —

CROYDON. Fuck it, what the —

BRILLIANT. Bloody glass is — *(The glass is spinning round wildly.)*

CROYDON. Come on — **Who's pushing it!**

FLUX *(broad Scot).* Something's tryin' ta get throo!

CROYDON. Bollocks.

FLUX. Will ye shut up! Somethin's tryin ta get throo!

CROYDON. Yeah, my houseboy!

BRILLIANT. What a struggle! Bloody glass is going mad!

CROYDON. Grow up, Flux, you bastard!

BRILLIANT. Awful struggle! Terrible struggle going on! Exhausting for the medium — don't think I can —

CROYDON. **Flux, what are you doing!**

FLUX *(in a vision).* It's for me! It's for me! Ask it is it for me!

CROYDON. Fucking nerve of him.

BRILLIANT. Is there a message for Archie, please? *(The glass hurtles to 'YES'.)* Yes.

CROYDON. Like hell there is.

BRILLIANT *(straining).* Gran - dad, Gran - dad it says —

FLUX. **Grandad?**

CROYDON. Come on, Archie; it's yer fucking grandad!

BRILLIANT. Keeps saying gran-dad, gran-dad —

CROYDON. Can we keep it witty because my arm is killing me.

BRILLIANT. Terrific struggle ... appealing to you ... gran-dad — gran-dad

FLUX *(perplexed).* Grandad?

BRILLIANT. What's this ... M ... 2 ... 3 ... M ... 2 ... 3 ... *(The glass slows down.)* Getting weaker ... struggle over ... M2 ... 3. *(The glass stops.)* That's it.

CROYDON *(removing his finger).* Thank Christ. Now can we agree on something. Not to fuck up one another's messages?

FLUX. Grandad — M what?

BRILLIANT.   2 — 3.

CROYDON.   Archie. Kindly do not fuck my messages.

BRILLIANT.   A stronger force seized control of the airwave.

CROYDON.   Yeah, well Archie always had a strong wrist, didn't you Archie?

BRILLIANT.   Possibly an act of censorship by more sensitive spirits. We were lucky the glass didn't shatter. I have known a glass to shatter.

FLUX.   Gettin' pissed off wi' your cock talk. Can scarcely blame 'em.

CROYDON.   Not my fault if the ether is packed with perverts, is it? All these bumboys getting a buzz in the fourth dimension. Crutch-huggers drifting in the stratosphere.

FLUX.   M23! It's a road of course. It's a motorway!

CROYDON *(looking at him).*   Oh dear, oh dear . . .

FLUX.   It's the road to Brighton, the M23!

CROYDON *(waving a finger).*   Archie . . . **Overdoing it** . . . okay?

FLUX *(looking at him indignantly).*   I'm looking for my gel! Do ye no see that? **I'm lookin' for my gel!** *(Pause. With embarrassment,* CROYDON *looks down into his lap.* BRILLIANT *begins collecting up the cards.)*

BRILLIANT.   Have a lot of fun with these. At Christmas. With the kiddies.

He wraps an elastic band round them, slips them in his pocket. An awkward silence elapses. He folds his arms, looks at the floor.

FLUX *(to* CROYDON*).*   Have ye ever had a daughter?

CROYDON.   Got no kids, Archie. You know that.

FLUX.   When ye have a kiddie —

CROYDON.   Can't do —

FLUX.   **When** ye have one —

CROYDON.   **Can't do. Archie! Lousy, rotten sperm count!** *(Long pause.)*

FLUX.   It's no like I ha' seen the body. Ye have seen people wi' lost kiddies. It's all right once they see the body. But I ha' seen nothin' for a whole rottin' year!

CROYDON.   Strain on a man . . .

FLUX.   Christ Jesus —

CROYDON.   I don't think I have shown a lack of sympathy.

FLUX.   I maybe have a message — I doon't knoo — but maybe the spirit of my gel is in tha' tumbler.

CROYDON.   Maybe.

FLUX.   It may sound stupid to ye. To ye I am a bloody idiot.

CROYDON.   I never said so.

FLUX.   But maybe the spirit of my gel is in the tumbler and ye canna prove to me she is na! Can ye? **Prove it!** *(*CROYDON *shrugs. He looks at* BRILLIANT.*)* Ye canna. *(Pause.)*

CROYDON.   Leave it there, shall we?

FLUX.   She is tryin ta get throo ta me! *(Long pause.)*

BRILLIANT.   I think it's Labour, don't you, Don?

CROYDON.   Labour, is it? I thought it was Moscow.

FLUX.   I ha' heard knockin' on my window . . .

CROYDON.   Five more years of communism. The English voter is a fucking masochist.

FLUX. I went out on the landing. There was nothin'. I went doonstairs an' there was nothin'.

BRILLIANT. Few more results to come through yet.

CROYDON. Fuck the Hebrides. The Reds are back.

FLUX. I went into the garden. There was nothin'.

CROYDON. We are supposed to be the police. We are supposed to be the guardians. And we witness the murder of our country. And we do nothing. I say what right have we to call ourselves the guardians?

FLUX. Nothin' but the knockin' . . . still the knockin' . . .

CROYDON. I cannot honestly say I am prepared to tolerate another five-year stint of it. Of England murder. Can you say that?

FLUX. Knockin' . . . knockin' . . .

CROYDON. Can you put your hand on your heart and say, I will sit back and take it? As a copper? As a guardian? Because I can't.

FLUX. **Hilary! Hilary!** I called out Hilary. I was out there in bare feet. But nothin'. Fuckin' nothin' *(Pause.)*

BRILLIANT. No. *(Pause.)* The answer to your question is no. *(They look at one another.)*

CROYDON. Did he hear that?

BRILLIANT. Not listening. *(They look at him.)* Is he?

Pause. They get up, go to the other table, pick up their caps and remove the gloves which are folded inside. CROYDON *taps* FLUX *lightly on the shoulder.*

CROYDON. Archie, it's gone midnight.

BRILLIANT *(inspired).* **Movement!**

CROYDON. What?

BRILLIANT. The Midnight Movement. Wha'd yer think? *(CROYDON nods seriously.)*

CROYDON. Home, Archie. Get tucked up.

FLUX. Thank ye . . .

CROYDON. They're locking up, old son.

He slips on his overcoat. BRILLIANT *carries his own across his arm. They go out. Pause.* FLUX *sits rigid in his chair. A girl in a blue overall enters, carrying a broom and a wastepaper bin. She drops the bin noisily.* FLUX *sits up.*

FLUX. Hilary . . .

JACKIE. Jackie.

FLUX. Hilary . . .

JACKIE. Jackie.

FLUX. Come to me, girl. Come on, come to me!

JACKIE. I'll just take the bin.

FLUX *(grinning).* Ye're very beautiful. By God, ye're very beautiful.

JACKIE. Don't you have a bin? *(She looks round quickly.)*

FLUX *(getting up).* Kiss me. Gi' me a kiss.

JACKIE. Oh, dear.

FLUX. Don't ye want ta kiss me, then?

JACKIE. Ta ta. *(She turns to go.)*

FLUX. **Stay where ye are!**

JACKIE *(amused by this command).* What?

FLUX. **Stay where ye are!**

JACKIE. No. *(She starts to go but* FLUX *rushes her, grabbing her clumsily.)* **Help! Help!**

FLUX. Ma gel! Ma gel! Ye're no leavin' me agin, I'll no have ye leavin' me agin!

JACKIE. **Police!**

FLUX. I got yer message, I knoo it was yoo!

JACKIE. **Somebody!**

FLUX. Oh, Jesus, lassie, can I no touch ye! *(*BRILLIANT *and* CROYDON *reappear. They struggle to pull* FLUX *away.)* Doon't let her gae! Doon't let her gae! She's my lassie. **Get yer hands off me!**

JACKIE. Ripped my sodding overall.

FLUX. My darlin'! My darlin'!

JACKIE. Seen too much of it, has he? Too much smut. Turned him.

CROYDON. Archie . . .

JACKIE. Last place you expect this sort of thing.

CROYDON. Cool it, Archie, cool it . . . *(Pause.* FLUX *gives up struggling. They stand back.)*

FLUX. **Fuck. Fuck.**

BRILLIANT. He isn't well.

JACKIE. I'm not feeling very well myself.

BRILLIANT. No, he isn't. Not at all well, is he?

CROYDON. Nope.

BRILLIANT. So if you'd —

JACKIE. I'm reporting it. *(They look at her.)* Sorry. I'm reporting it.

CROYDON. What are you reporting?

JACKIE. I was assaulted. *(They look at her.)* Well, wasn't I?

BRILLIANT. Technically.

CROYDON. **He assaulted her.**

BRILLIANT *(with a shrug).* All right, he assaulted you.

JACKIE. So can I report it, please? *(Pause.)* Well, can I please! *(Pause.)*

CROYDON. Get a charge sheet, Brian, please . . . *(*BRILLIANT *goes out.* CROYDON *looks at* FLUX.*)* Fucked yer pension up, ol' fruit . . .

Lights fade to black.

Scene Three

A rusty iron bed. FINNEY *is sitting on the springs.*

FINNEY. We had a Horlicks. I said I would make the Horlicks but she said no, because of the election she would do it. At this time the Swingometer showed a net gain to the Tories of 30 seats. She brought me my Horlicks and went upstairs. She was reading *The Gentle Monarch*, the life of George VI. She loved biographies. If she did not read she could not sleep. Just a few lines and she would be dozing. I envied that because I sleep so badly. I had asked for tablets but the doctor didn't want to as I drink so much. She said it was the wallpaper, but how can wallpaper make you sleep badly, because you shut your eyelids when you sleep. I thought that was a silly argument.

ERICA *comes in, dragging a filthy mattress. She drops it, contemplates it.*

ERICA.   Imagine the germs there are in that. Imagine the piss that has soaked into it. Gallons of incontinence. People have died on that, I bet. That has seen more suffering than the sharp end of an enema. *(Pause. She looks at him.)* Shall we stick it on, then? Or do you like to kip on rusty springs?

FINNEY *(getting up, lifting an end of the mattress).*   What sort of hospital was this?

ERICA.   Isolation. They shut it as a social spending cut.

FINNEY.   What diseases?

ERICA.   TB. When the wind blows you can hear 'em coughin'. Every inch of floor and ceiling has the stain of someone's spit. *(They lift the mattress onto the bed.)* Do you wanna pillow?

FINNEY.   I don't think so.

ERICA.   Chicken *(She starts to go.)*

FINNEY.   I have hardly has a day's illness. I have never missed a day at work.

ERICA.   Well, Rule Britannia. *(She goes out.)*

FINNEY.   The pony. I was thinking of the pony. What it costs. For fodder and for stabling. And the vet's expenses and the kit. Upstairs the twins were dreaming ponies. I had continually put them off. They kept on that their friends had got them, they said that they would prefer it to a private school. I came to hate the sight of ponies, the sound of hooves would make me shut the window. This came over me while they announced the Greater Manchester results. I have a shotgun but I can't afford the cartridges. I don't go shooting though my friends have asked me to. I have no social life. *(ERICA comes in with some thick, grimy material.)*

ERICA.   If you hang this across the window you can have a light on. Otherwise not. Because over there's a farmhouse and if they see us they'll have the coppers on us. *(She drops it in a heap.)*

FINNEY.   You never see the police? They don't call in?

ERICA.   Got no need to. This place is protected.

FINNEY.   Who by?

ERICA.   The Leopard Security Co. The leopard is Mr Rutkin, but we never see him 'cos he's scared of germs. He looks through the gates sometimes, if the wind's in his favour.

FINNEY.   God, I am so cold.

ERICA   That's the trouble with this place. Too bloody airy. If you got lung-rot they always stick you in a draught. We hate medicine, Hilary an' me. We're doing without it.

FINNEY.   No blankets, I suppose.

ERICA.   Sorry.

FINNEY.   **Freezing.**

ERICA.   They left two hundred mattresses but not a single blanket. I expect they wanted them to infect some tribe. *(She starts to go out.)* I'm makin' cocoa if you want it. *(She stops, turns.)* They found the motor. *(He doesn't react.)* They found your jag. *(Pause.)* **Killer's car. Dead infant quiz.** *(Pause.)*

That's the Express. *(She waits for him to speak. But he is silent.)* You were
right. It is a Labour government. *(She goes out. Long pause.)*

FINNEY.   All through the sixties I had asked them for a partnership. I began
to think I would never get a partnership, then suddenly last year they called
me in and offered me a partnership. The thing is that a partner has no salary.
But they said it was a gesture of their confidence in me. After that I only got
commission. We were living in the country. We had got a place near
Godalming. We had seen Churchill's studio at Chartwell with his cigar and
his whisky just like he was coming in. Jeniffer paints like Churchill so we had
built this studio. **Then the market started sliding.** First we sacked the
messengers. Old boys past retirement age. Then some of the juniors. Then all
of them. I was doing my own typing. Letters to investors with two fingers.
Last year I eaned **Two thousand pounds.** She drinks Campari, I drink
Scotch. Our drink bill was nine hundred pounds and school fees have gone
up. **Labour wants to kill our type!** *(Pause.)* I came home, sat down, got the
bottle out. I did not speak. Whole evenings and I did not speak. Had dinner in
the kitchen by myself. She started locking herself in the studio. One night I
went down with some bricks. Broke all her windows. Kids were crying. Fell
down in the orchard. Peed myself. She begged me would I see a specialist. I
said how could I, we had dropped out of the Health Insurance scheme **and
then the Swingometer went into the red!** *(Pause.)* Red is the colour of the
Labour Party and of Communism and when I looked I saw it was the colour
of the cartridges. **Symbolical.** *(Pause.)* I heard the government had put out
tenders for forced labour camps. *(ERICA comes in, stands for a moment.)*

ERICA.   I was just thinkin' . . . *(He looks up.)* Why didn't you shoot yerself?
(Pause. He stares.) Silly question, I suppose . . .

FINNEY.   Only had four cartridges.

ERICA.   Yeah. *(Pause.)* Well, that's —

FINNEY.   One each.

ERICA.   Exactly. *(Long pause.)*

FINNEY.   The dog.

ERICA.   The dog.

FINNEY.   Spaniel.

ERICA.   Ah. *(Pause. She grins.)* Oh, well, that's it, then. Just that Hilary was
wondering —

FINNEY.   It came in. Just after I had . . . the twins.

ERICA.   Drag.

FINNEY.   From the kitchen. It slept in the kitchen. It was the runt of a litter.
All the rest were gun dogs. But Topper wasn't any good. Used to run to the
gun. Instead of to the target.

ERICA.   Stupid animal. *(She turns to go.)* We were only wondering —

FINNEY.   **What is the matter with you people!**

ERICA *(looking at him).* Nothin'. *(Pause. He glares at her.)* Well, Hilary says
it's the bankruptcy of Humanitarianism. If I got it right. Or is it Humanism?
One of them. *(He just stares at her.)* You do mean that, do you? You mean
why don't we wet our knickers when a mass murderer walks in? You mean
how could we leave a dead baby in a stranger's car? *(Pause.)* **Is that what you
mean!**

FINNEY.   Labour has done that. It's Labour, isn't it?

ERICA.   I used to keep hamsters as a kid. When one died or got trod on, my
dad bought me another one. So I got to know a lot of hamsters. And they
were all different. Some built good nests, some built lousy ones. Some could
climb up the curtains and some could hardly climb at all. And some bit you
and some didn't. They were all individuals. They were like human beings.
Every one was different. And yet there I was, treading on 'em. And I knew
that what was true of hamsters had to be true of rats as well. Every rat that
ever lived was **unique** — and **every ant!** *(Pause.)* You have to keep it in
perspective. The fact that we are different doesn't make us valuable. There's
too much fuss about this precious fucking **human life.** *(Pause.* FINNEY *is
horrified.)* You should talk to Hilary. She's good on that. She says — hold it
— hold it — 'Respect for human life is the rock on which they built the status
quo.' **Got it!** *(She grins. Pause.)* First time I've got that. Do you love language? I do. Though Hilary's got a thing about that. She says it's — fuck it —
no, it's gone . . . Somethin' anyway. Did you want a cocoa? *(He just stares.)*
You should talk more. *(She turns. Goes a little way, stops. Inspired.)* 'The
sledgehammer of social conformity!' Or conformism, is it? That's it, anyway.
(He doesn't react.) **Language.** *(She carries on her way.)* Cocoas in the
operating theatre. *(She grins.)* It really was. Lung tissue in all the teacups.

She goes out. Pause. Then FINNEY *rips his tie off, undoes the neck of his shirt,
makes a noose of his tie and puts it over his head. He holds the other end above
his head, looking urgently for a place to hang it. As he hurries about the room,
there comes the sound of a cough, a repetitive, tubercular cough.* FINNEY *stops,
uneasy. The coughing comes nearer, preceding the appearance of the spectre of
an inmate. Thin, stooping and in hospital pyjamas, it stops in front of him,
coughing, looking at the floor.*

SPECTRE.   This was my room. What are you doing in my room?
FINNEY.   I want to hang myself. But there are no hooks.
SPECTRE.   They used ter do it from the lockers.
FINNEY.   Yes, but —
SPECTRE.   Where are the lockers?
FINNEY.   I don't know. I'm new here.
SPECTRE.   **What have they done with my locker!**
FINNEY.   Probably a job lot.
SPECTRE.   I left a postcard in my locker! Has anybody seen my locker?
FINNEY.   Postcard?
SPECTRE.   I was shouting but they could not hear me! Bury it with me, I told
'em. **They should not inject you when you try to speak!**
FINNEY.   What was on it?
SPECTRE.   Stole it.
FINNEY.   Who did?
SPECTRE.   **Doctor. Stole it.** *(He breaks into coughing again. His shoulders
shake. Pause.)*
FINNEY.   What did it say?
SPECTRE.   Get Well Soon. Yours, King George VI.
FINNEY.   That's nice . . .
SPECTRE.   Came to my bedside. With a piece of gauze across his mouth.
Shook hands. Gave me a postcard with a picture of himself. It was on my

locker. I was the first to die in here. He had weak lungs but **He still came here.** His bastard brother always in the newspapers. Going down the coal-mines in white suits. Something must be done. The liar! **Would he have come here?** *(*FINNEY *shrugs his shoulders.)* Are you **Finney**?

FINNEY.   Yes.

SPECTRE.   I am to tell you there is nothing satisfactory in death. Your lungs are healthy.

FINNEY.   England's changed since your day.

SPECTRE.   It is a bed of nails to you.

FINNEY.   I have thought of dying.

SPECTRE.   Is it a bed of nails to you?

FINNEY.   Yes, so I thought of dying!

SPECTRE.   Wrong answer. I'll ask again. Is it a bed of nails to you?

FINNEY.   Yes!

SPECTRE.   Then set your mind to changing it.

FINNEY.   I think I prefer the other —

SPECTRE.   **Finney** you have a problem. You are **Weak**.

FINNEY.   Yes.

SPECTRE.   You admit it.

FINNEY.   I admit it.

SPECTRE.   Proudly.

FINNEY.   I know myself.

SPECTRE.   **Weak.** It is a symptom of weakness that it claims to know itself.

FINNEY.   Possibly, I have been under awful —

SPECTRE.   **There is an alien presence!**

FINNEY.   They're in the operating-room, they won't —

SPECTRE.   **There is an alien presence!**Finney, you are to help our people —

FINNEY.   Our people?

SPECTRE.   **The English!** You are to help the **English!**

FINNEY.   I'd like to die, can't I just die?

SPECTRE.   Struggle the hardest when things look the worst. Nothing is certain. Nothing is lost. At the head of the stairs a loose runner brings a fatal fall.

FINNEY.   What . . . ?

SPECTRE.   **Bugger! Are you listening?**

FINNEY.   Sorry.

SPECTRE *(coughing again).*   Got to go now. Alien presence, sod it. Got to go.

He glides away, coughing. FINNEY *watches him go out. Suddenly there comes the sound of loud, constricted breathing, played over speakers.* FINNEY *looks over his shoulder, then scrambles under the bed. A man appears wearing a crash helmet and a wartime rubber gas-mask. He has a leather jacket bearing the emblem of the Leopard Security Company on the back. He is carrying a can of petrol. He looks quickly out of the door, then starts sprinkling petrol all over the floor. The sound of his breathing in the mask continues throughout. At last he tosses the can aside and takes a rag out of his hip pocket. He is about to put a lighter to it when* ERICA *appears with a mug of cocoa.*

ERICA.   **Hil — ary!**

The man drops the rag and grabs a cosh from his other pocket, adopting a defensive posture. His attempt to speak, which come out as indistinct grunts, also come through the speakers.

RUTKIN.   Ooo — ah — yoo!

ERICA.   **Hil — ary!**

RUTKIN.   Ooo — ah — yoo! Ooo — ah — yoo!

FINNEY *(making an appearance).*   It's all right, I'm —

ERICA.   Well, what the —

FINNEY.   I was just — I was —

RUTKIN.   On't — moov — On't — moov — Eider — o — yoo — **On't moov!**

ERICA.   Mr Rutkin, I presume.

RUTKIN.   **Priva - prop — ery! Tre — pass - in!**

ERICA.   Arsonist.

RUTKIN *(furiously).*   **I — not — I not!**

ERICA.   Fucking little arsonist.

RUTKIN.   **I — not — I — not!**

HILARY *(appearing in a dressing-gown).*   Take that stupid mask off.

RUTKIN *(shaking his head).*   **Nev — er!**

HILARY.   The germs are dead, Rutkin.

RUTKIN *(laughing mockingly).*   Yoo'd like me to believe — *(She takes a step towards him)* **Geh — back! Geh — back!**

HILARY.   I have just had a baby. You can't hit me.

RUTKIN *(stepping back himself).*   **Don't — come — don't —**

HILARY.   People don't hit maternity cases. We have an aura, you see. *(She takes a step nearer.)* No predator will touch an animal that has just dropped a litter. *(She takes another.)* Take the mask off Rutkin.

RUTKIN.   **Geh — away — please — geh —**

Suddenly HILARY *and* ERICA *grab* RUTKIN *and pull off his gas mask. He screams, then appears to choke, clutching his throat.*

HILARY.   Well, breathe, then. *(Pause.)* You've got to breathe. *(They watch as he splutters on the floor.)*

FINNEY.   No, he isn't. *(He looks at the girls.)* Is he. *(Pause.)* He's not —

RUTKIN *(gulping for air).*   **You killed me!**

HILARY.   Why do you want to burn down people's homes?

RUTKIN.   **Poisoned me!**

HILARY.   Why are you so fucking destructive? **We live here.** *(He looks at* HILARY, *amazed.)*

ERICA.   Rutkin. Answer Hilary.

RUTKIN *(mumbling).*   Crops.

ERICA.   What?

RUTKIN.   **Crops!** Ruined the crops.

HILARY.   Idiot.

RUTKIN.   **Has ruined the crops!** *(Pause. He regains his breath.)* Best potato land in Sussex till they stuck this here. Soil's full of germs now. Nothing grows. **Half dead people from the towns stuck here, wha'd' you expect?** *(Pause.)* The air's gone black.

ERICA. Black air?

HILARY. First I've heard of it.

RUTKIN. Not local, are yer? Wouldn't know. At sunset you can see black air. Hanging over this place. Watch it from the Green Man. **Filthy air!**

HILARY. You are a pathetic bumpkin. You are rotten with superstition.

RUTKIN *(with a flash of realization).* **I can't go near my family now!**

ERICA. Plenty of rooms here.

RUTKIN. Can never kiss my little girl. **My breath is dirty!**

ERICA. We got loads of mattresses.

RUTKIN. I can't go home . . . I can't go home . . .

HILARY. If you like I will explain why you cannot possibly be a TB carrier. It is called science.

RUTKIN. **You can't! You can't!**

HILARY. Ah. I rather thought so.

RUTKIN. Science is shit. It brings filthy people out of cities and sticks 'em in the middle of our fields. It's shit!

ERICA. I reckon Rutkin's into magic. I think he digs up corpses and buggers his missus on a gravestone.

RUTKIN. How dare you!

ERICA. You're a bit of a goblin, aren't yer? You and yer black air.

FINNEY. I don't think we are helping him. I think we might be making him worse. *(They look at him.)* It seems to me.

ERICA. Well, what do you suggest we do?*(Pause.)*

HILARY. We could always murder him. *(They turn to her.)* Well, couldn't we?

ERICA. Got a bleeding expert, haven't we?

RUTKIN. **I wouldn't be the first one.** There were hearses leaving this place twice a day. **Twice a day.** Try bringing up a kiddie in a place like this.

HILARY. I was intending to.

RUTKIN *(staring at her).* Mad bitch. Mad bloody bitch.

HILARY. What makes you so tedious, Rutkin, is your clammy panic. You are sweaty with terrors. Your miserable little cranium is a boiling cocktail of ignorance and crap —

ERICA. **Great!**

HILARY. You are a compost heap of undigested rumours. You are a fucking great bucolic belch!

RUTKIN. Wha'?

HILARY. Why is it someone always comes along and **fucks you up!***(Pause.)*

RUTKIN. I never knew anybody lived here. I never knew.

FINNEY. I read there was a family living in a council rubbish chute.

ERICA. Can't empty yer bin in case it stifles somebody.

RUTKIN. Don't read the papers . . .

ERICA. Labour is the government.

HILARY. Get the car round.

ERICA. What?

HILARY. Get the car round.

ERICA. But what do we —

HILARY. Finished here. Obviously finished here.

ERICA.   Only if he —
HILARY.   **What is our rule?***(Pause.)*
ERICA.   Rule . . . Rule . . .
HILARY.   **Our fucking rule!**
ERICA *(in a flash)*. At the first sign of a struggle — Quit.
HILARY.   Then get the car round. *(ERICA goes out. Pause.)*
FINNEY.   It's funny, but actually I . . . I loathe this. This sort of living. I loathe
  it.
HILARY.   Miss the gin and tonic.
FINNEY.   The aimlessness.*(Pause.)* Disturbs me. *(Pause.)* Disgusts me.
  (Pause.) No offence. *(Pause.)* It's funny, but —
HILARY.   It's not funny.
FINNEY.   No.
HILARY.   Nothing funny in it.
FINNEY.   I just thought if I didn't like it, I could go back.
HILARY.   And do you want to?
FINNEY.   At the moment.*(Pause.)*
HILARY.   Where were you going? When we stopped you?
FINNEY.   Nowhere.*(Pause.)*
HILARY.   Get your coat on, Finney.

Sound of a car stopping outside. HILARY *goes out.* FINNEY *picks up his city
overcoat, puts it on, watched by*RUTKIN. *He is about to go, but stops. Looks at*
RUTKIN.

FINNEY.   I have a feeling I am going to suffer.

*Pause.*RUTKIN *just looks at him. He goes out. More car sounds, then it drives
away.*RUTKIN *is about to get up when he sees something lying under the bed.
He recovers it, examines it. It is a postcard.*

RUTKIN.   Finney. Cherry Cottage. Godalming.

*He looks at it for some seconds, then taking the lighter out of his pocket, makes it
into a spill. He drops it on the floor. Blackout as he runs out.*

Scene Four

*A London Park at midnight. A bench. A panorama of the city's twinkling
lights.*CROYDON, *hands thrust deep in his overcoat pockets, is walking up and
down. He stops, staring into the view. He climbs onto the bench. Pause.*

CROYDON.   Every light is somebody. Every flicker is a family in its smelly
  little room. A dockyard crane. A train. The stairwell of a council block. The
  car door opening as a bloke says goodnight to a tart. A streetlamp where a
  dog is pissing or a gang of louts are scuffing and decent people are too scared
  to pass. Cold lavatories in slums or plushy bedrooms on a smart estate.
  Wicker basket lampshade or a naked bulb. Blacks and whites and
  communists. All lights are people. And all of 'em are blacked out by **one**

switch. *(He turns away. As he does so the park clock tolls midnight. After a few strokes,* BRILLIANT *comes in, wearing a duffle coat with the hood up.)*

BRILLIANT.   Sorry I'm late, they — *(*CROYDON *silences him with a hand. The clock completes its chimes.)* Sorry I'm late. They shut the gates.
CROYDON.   So how did you get in?
BRILLIANT.   Showed my card.
CROYDON.   Who to?
BRILLIANT.   The keeper. At the lodge.
CROYDON.   You told the bloody keeper who you were?
BRILLIANT.   I couldn't have climbed, Don. have you seen the gates?
CROYDON.   I seen 'em and I climbed 'em.
BRILLIANT.   You play sport.
CROYDON.   So the keeper knows we're here?
BRILLIANT.   Me not we.
CROYDON.   So much for our privacy.
BRILLIANT.   We are private, Don —
CROYDON.   **Wass that!**
BRILLIANT.   Nothing.
CROYDON.   **Shh!** *(Pause.)*
BRILLIANT.   I tell —
CROYDON.   **Shh!** *(Pause.* BRILLIANT *walks up and down, stops.)*
BRILLIANT.   I told him there was a gang of kids out here. He won't come out. *(Pause.)* Out of interest. What are we doing here? *(Pause.)* Why this spot in particular. When there are others. Cars and so on. *(Pause.)* Don.
CROYDON.   Because of that *(He nods towards the lights.)*
BRILLIANT.   What?
CROYDON.   **That!** *(Pause.)*
BRILLIANT.   Can't see it, sorry.
CROYDON.   **Lon — don.**
BRILLIANT.   Oh.
CROYDON.   And that's not all of it.
BRILLIANT.   No. *(Pause.)*
CROYDON.   Look at it.
BRILLIANT.   Yup.
CROYDON.   I want us to come here often. I want us to make a thing of it. To bring the kids here. Have a picnic. I want to make a fetish of it. I want you and me to sit here late at night, with coffee and a sandwich. Can you think why? *(Pause.)*
BRILLIANT.   Not exactly —
CROYDON.   Because we must be certain. And that view tells me two things at once. How **big** it is. And how **easy** it is.
BRILLIANT.   Yes.
CROYDON.   So look at it and tell me. Do we go on? *(Pause.)*
BRILLIANT.   What do you think?
CROYDON.   You tell me. Stand up on the bench and then tell me. *(*BRILLIANT *climbs onto the bench and looks out.)* Every light is somebody. Every flicker is a family in its stuffy little room. All lights are people. And all of 'em are blacked out by **one switch**. *(Pause.)* My point being that

when it comes to getting rid of governments, people are apt to **exaggerate**.
BRILLIANT.   Yup.
CROYDON.   They think it is too complex, when the complexities of our
world have made it simpler. They think it is too ambitious, when it is simply
that their imaginations are too small. It is a question of getting your finger on
the switch. *(Pause.)*
BRILLIANT.   Yup. *(Pause.)*
CROYDON.   **Do you want to?** *(Pause. Then* BRILLIANT *steps down.)*
BRILLIANT.   How much violence would there be?
CROYDON.   Need be very little.
BRILLIANT.   I ask because I have a family.
CROYDON.   Understandable.
BRILLIANT.   And in a revolution kids get —
CROYDON.   Nope.
BRILLIANT.   Get killed.
CROYDON.   Nope. Nope. *(Pause.)* Listen. I never said a revolution. I am
thinking more about a coup. Because I am not asking for changes, which is
what a revolution does. I am asking for a stop. I am not asking for a rising of
the herd because that means destruction. That means damage. It means a
fucking great big snowball which ends up rolling through your house. I am
asking for a few good men. You, for example.
BRILLIANT.   Yup.
CROYDON.   I am still at the discussion stage.
BRILLIANT.   Yup.
CROYDON.   And I show you that view because I want to simplify the issue. I
do not want us to get befogged. Because this is dear old England people have
got the idea nothing changes except through the cogs and gears. I say that is
not so. I say you could wake up with a different geezer at the top and the
sodding engine would still run. And it would not require much violence. I
don't want to be unduly optimistic but it might need none at all.
BRILLIANT.   I think that's optimistic.
CROYDON.   We are entitled to be, Brian.
BRILLIANT.   The thought of children being hurt upsets me.
CROYDON.   They won't be.
BRILLIANT.   I think they will. I think you're underplaying it.
CROYDON.   We're not a mass movement, are we? You and me?
BRILLIANT.   Hardly.
CROYDON.   And in the interests of the kiddies it's a good thing we are not.
Because it is mass movements that get the kiddies killed. Compare the
Russian revolution with Richard III.
BRILLIANT.   He murdered the little princes!
CROYDON.   Fucking hell, Brian, we can't stop history because we happen to
have kids! Kids are only baby adults. *(Pause.)*
BRILLIANT.   You see, you haven't got one. I don't think you'd say that if you
had one.
CROYDON.   They are playing on your sentiments. Can't you see that? They
rely on your wonderful humanity not to lift a finger. Meanwhile they're
pissing over England. I tell you, Brian, in a few years this place will be as big a
shit-heap as sodding Bangladesh. Get yer priorities right, or we are getting

nowhere! *(Pause. He stalks up and down.)* I want to act. I want to act in concert with a tiny band. I am convinced the morning after everybody will just go to work. It's human nature. If you study history you will find people do that. They just get up and go to work.

BRILLIANT.   I don't know a lot of history.

CROYDON.   Study it.

BRILLIANT.   I will do. But I — if I might — I personally wonder if I am actually — intelligent enough. To run Great Britain. With all respect. I don't think we are intellectual. Either of us. *(Pause.)*

CROYDON.   Brian, I had no idea you were such a victim of the myth.

BRILLIANT.   What myth?

CROYDON.   The myth they use to blind you with. The myth that governing is an art. The myth that the governor of the Bank of England is anything but a stinking fart. That Mrs Thatcher is anything but a vapour cloud of perfumed cretinism. Or Benn a screaming sycophant. That bosses do things that the workers can't. That surgeons are parties to magic and economists are on familiar terms with God. It's shit and trickery, Brian, and you have filled your guts with it! *(Pause.)*

BRILLIANT.   I must read more history.

CROYDON.   How is it that some drunken homosexual of a minister can run the hospitals one day and the fucking air force on the next? How is it? Ask yerself!

BRILLIANT.   Dunno.

CROYDON.   **Do know! Do know!**

BRILLIANT.   I suppose . . . I suppose . . .

CROYDON.   **Think. Think.**

BRILLIANT.   They — somebody — somebody else —

CROYDON.   **Somebody else!** Always **somebody else**. It's a machine. It runs without a leader. It is hundreds of years old and it runs smooth as a sleeve-valve, up and down, up and down. It is a beautiful sight and it could be commanded by a **rabbit**. Do you follow?

BRILLIANT.   Yup.

CROYDON.   All that matters is that every little man who serves it, the bald-headed geezer with the mortgage and the shiny arse, turns up to the office. On that morning. That he persists. And he will, Brian, because not to do so is an effort and calls for thought, which he would prefer not to burden himself with. And the more days that pass the less likely he is to act, because it would cause chaos and **his kids might be hurt**. History is the history of dedicated individuals. Do you see? *(Long pause.* BRILLIANT *walks up and down, stops.)*

BRILLIANT.   Feel my hand.

CROYDON.   Why?

BRILLIANT.   Go on. Feel my hand. *(He extends it.* CROYDON *touches it.)* Gone cold. I only get that when I'm acting as a medium. But I got it then, listening to you. *(Pause.)* It sort of froze. *(Pause.)*

CROYDON.   Well . . .

BRILLIANT.   Funny. *(Pause.)* Ought to be going, I think.

CROYDON.   Gone half past twelve.

BRILLIANT.   Your missus will be wondering . . .

CROYDON.   Doubt it. *(Pause.)* Same place next week?

BRILLIANT.   I don't think we've got anything —

CROYDON.   Climb over next time. Do you good.

BRILLIANT.   All right. I'll try. *(He turns to go.)* Suppose we best leave
separately.

CROYDON *makes a gesture of indifference.* BRILLIANT *goes out.*
CROYDON *looks into the lights of London. He hears a cough behind him.*
Spins round.

CROYDON.   **Who's there! Come on, who's there!**

METHS *(an Irish accent).*   'Ol right, 'ol right —

CROYDON.   Where are yer! I can't see yer!

METHS.   'Ol right, 'ol right! *(A vagrant appears out of the shadows.)*

CROYDON.   Who are you? What are you doing here?

METHS.   I live here. Yer on my seat.

CROYDON.   What have you heard?

METHS.   Most of it.

CROYDON.   That was a private fucking conversation! Christ, there is hardly
room to stand up in this country! What did you hear?

METHS.   Nothin' I ain't heard before. *(Pause.)* They all come here. Stand on
my seat. The young ones talk about women an' the old ones about the
government.

CROYDON.   I'm not old.

METHS.   No offence to yer. I hev heard an old bloke talk about a tart. He took
his doodle out. Stiff as a brick. Stood there an' said, 'London be my witness,
this will lie in Hilary ternight!' Smart old geezer, in a camel overcoat.

CROYDON.   Filth.

METHS.   You hear the lot here. I had thought of movin' but it's an education.
Got a fag?

CROYDON.   Don't smoke.

METHS.   Give us a bob an' I'll tell yer what I think of yer.

CROYDON.   Full of liberties, aren't you, son? *(Pause, then he dips in his
pocket, hands over a coin.* METHS *pockets it. Pause, then deliberately and
gravely.)*

METHS.   The Organ-ized Wor-kers. *(Pause.)*

CROYDON.   What about 'em?

METHS.   Won't sit still, will they? They itch like piles.

CROYDON.   Yeah. An' that's all they do do. Fingers always at their bums.
All friction, no satisfaction. What else?

METHS.   Nothin' else. *(Pause.)*

CROYDON.   Robbery.

METHS *(shrugs).*   Jest warnin' yer.

CROYDON.   How about the lumpenproletariat?

METHS.   Yeh, well, that's another thing.

CROYDON.   Urban bourgeois?

METHS.   Could be . . .

CROYDON.   Ragbag. Ragbag of useless phraseology.

METHS.   I hev ter make a living, don't I? *(The clock chimes the half hour.
Pause.)*

CROYDON.   Where are yer? *(He looks side to side.* METHS *has vanished.* CROYDON *climbs back on the bench, faces London. He appears to be altering his clothing. There is a sound of urinating.)* London, through the steaming torrent of my piss I vow . . . *(Pause.)* No I don't. Only an idiot makes promises.

Blackout.

Scene Five

A dockland warehouse. A heap of sacks, very dim lighting. A torch flashes sporadically. ERICA *is calling.*

ERICA.   Light switch . . . **Light switch** . . .
HILARY.   Keep it still, then!
ERICA.   **Echo! Echo!**
HILARY.   Can we concentrate on the light switch?
ERICA.   **E-cho!**
HILARY.   Oh, fuck, Erica.
ERICA.   Smelly. Very smelly. *(They appear, followed by* FINNEY.*)*
HILARY.   Go that way. Follow the wall.
ERICA.   **Felt a rat!**
HILARY.   Never.
ERICA.   **Fuckin' rat!**
HILARY.   Finney will go that way. We will go this way.
FINNEY.   What for?
HILARY.   Bloody light switch.
FINNEY.   Don't want the light.
HILARY/ERICA.   **Oh Christ . . .**
FINNEY.   Don't want anything.
HILARY.   Sit down.
FINNEY.   Don't want to.
HILARY.   **Sit down.** *(He wanders to the sacks. Sits on them.)* Erica. Keep walking and you come to a switch. Go on.
ERICA *(going off, groping).*   Nope . . .
HILARY.   Keep going . . . *(Suddenly the lights come on.)*
ERICA/HILARY.   Did you do that? *(Pause.)* Nope. *(*ERICA *reappears, looks at* HILARY, *shrugs.)*
HILARY.   Illumination by sympathy. The electric impulse of our intimacy has activated the filament.
ERICA.   Nightwatchman.
HILARY.   Isn't one.
ERICA.   How do you know?
HILARY.   I've been here and there isn't one.
ERICA *(with a shrug).*   Lovely 'ol place . . . *(She wanders about.)* They built better warehouses than homes. Those ol' sacks were better taken care of than most people. What does a sack want with a gothic winder?

HILARY.   Venetian.

ERICA.   Sorry.

HILARY.   Round top.

ERICA.   Sorry.

HILARY.   The aesthetics of speculation. They couldn't disentangle art and profit. The spiritual disease of the nineteenth century is symbolized by the urge to put Corinthian capitals on workhouses.

ERICA.   Correct. *(Pause.)* I like it though. I feel posh.

FINNEY.   I want to give myself up.

ERICA.   Balls.

FINNEY.   There are all these people looking for me, and it is horrible in here. I am giving myself up.

ERICA.   You don't want to give yourself up. You are being dramatic. Stop showing off.

HILARY.   You only want to give yourself up because all murderers give themselves up. You are being manipulated.

FINNEY.   I am not a murderer.

HILARY.   Sorry.

FINNEY.   You keep calling me a murderer.

HILARY.   I am sorry.

FINNEY.   I want to tell them why I did it.

HILARY.   We know why you did it.

FINNEY.   Yes, but they think I'm dishonest! I want to be **honest**. *(Pause.)*

HILARY.   Yes . . .

FINNEY.   Why can't I be honest? *(Pause.)*

ERICA.   I'll get the stuff in, shall I? Maybe tomorrow we can get a door going. I don't like climbing in at winders. *(She goes out.* HILARY *sits next to* FINNEY *on the sacks.)*

HILARY.   Do you know something? This is where it happened. On these sacks. The actual, same, identical sacks. *(Pause. He just looks at her.)* If you look you might see little dusty, human stains . . . *(She examines the sacks.)* My stains. *(Pause.)* His stains. *(Pause.)* This is where it happened, Finney. This is where I got **done up**. *(Pause.)*

FINNEY.   Would you mind if I went to the police?

HILARY.   I'm telling you something!

FINNEY.   I know. I'm sorry but I —

HILARY.   You are always going on about yourself! What **you** have done. It is very boring what **you** have done. You go on about it like you discovered relativity.

FINNEY.   Sorry.

HILARY.   It is very touching but as you say and keep on saying **It is done.** *(Pause. He stares at her.)* Now listen to what I've done. *(Pause.)* Like getting knocked up on this sack. And who did it. Because it was on this sack my baby was conceived. Or more precisely in my womb, but I was lying on this sack at the time. Are you interested? *(He looks embarassed.)*

FINNEY.   Yes.

HILARY.   You are.

FINNEY.   Yes.

HILARY.   I don't know why I'm telling you. Erica doesn't know this, and

Erica knows everything. I think I'm telling you because I believe in intimacy and I want you to know something about me like I know something about you. All right?

FINNEY.   Thank you.

HILARY.   Okay, then. He was an old geezer and he owns this warehouse. He and my father are Rotarians. I had known him on and off since I was six. One night last year he came round on a visit. I think he must have been on heat because he was looking at me with a kind of fishy eye. There is nothing quite so disgusting as an old man with a fishy eye, but I had decided not to be disgusted. I can do that. I can extinguish my aesthetics with my will. I could eat shit if I needed to. Anyway, my father being momentarily out of the room, he put his hand on my hand and then took my hand to his cock. What do you think of that? An old geezer of 65. And I thought if he wants it, why don't I give it to him, and I squeezed his trousers in return. Because once you have given something it isn't difficult to give the lot. Does that disgust you?

FINNEY.   Yes.

HILARY.   He was going red with disbelief. When he said meet me at the park gates he could barely get the words out. It was like his tongue had got too big. My father offered him a tablet, thinking he had heart disease.

FINNEY *stares at her.* ERICA *comes in laden with blankets and sleeping bags.*

ERICA.   Before the fish and chip shop shuts, can I make a suggestion? *(*HILARY *looks at her.)* Can I? *(She looks from one to the other.)* Can I or not?

HILARY *(ignoring her).*   I'm not on the pill. I don't believe in flooding my veins with chemicals. I'm not on the coil. I don't believe in copper suppurating in my womb. I was down to good intentions. He bought me a tenth-rate curry in the High Road and then brought me here. He went on about the romance of old buildings. I saw his neck was getting red. I thought if he does it to me I'll get pregnant. And if he made me pregnant I knew I would have it. And he did. And I was. *(Pause.)*

ERICA.   What's this?

HILARY.   Acquiesence in Cosmic Inevitability.

ERICA.   I fancy cod.

HILARY.   Letting Mother Nature grab the controls. Sort of uterine hi-jack.

ERICA.   They shut at ten. *(*HILARY *gets up, brushes herself down.)*

HILARY.   Down the chip bar, Finney. *(He doesn't move.)*

ERICA.   Come on Finney. Got to eat. *(They move off, wait for him.)*

HILARY.   He's not coming.

ERICA.   **Come on!**

HILARY.   He's not coming because he is offended. Something I said offended him.

FINNEY.   I'm not hungry.

ERICA.   **You are hungry.**

FINNEY.   I'm not. Really I'm not.

HILARY.   He is offended in his **values.** It has killed his appetite.

FINNEY.   **I'm just not hungry!**

ERICA *(going out).*   Bring yer back a bit of cod.

They go out. Silence. Then a sound of a tubercular cough. FINNEY *gets up. Enter the* SPECTRE *of the hospital inmate, shuffling.*

SPECTRE.   I used to work here. I was a storeman in 192— **Sod it!** There is an alien presence.
FINNEY.   Listen —
SPECTRE *(moving off again).*   I can't —
FINNEY.   I have a feeling which I think —
SPECTRE *(coughing).*   Can't stop.
FINNEY.   I don't think is decent —
SPECTRE.   Can't stop —
FINNEY.   **Is it decent for a man like me!**

The SPECTRE *just goes out, coughing.* FINNEY *stands, confused. Comes an echo of a heavy door closing and voices.* FINNEY *grabs up the sleeping bags and chucks them behind the sacks, then follows after. Suddenly the lights go out.*

GLORIA.   Christ!
NATTRESS.   Sorry.
GLORIA.   What you —
NATTRESS.   Sorry —
GLORIA.   Turn the lights off for? *(They come on again.)*
NATTRESS.   Must have been on already.
GLORIA.   Spooked me.
NATTRESS.   Scared you. Sorry. *(They are standing in the warehouse.* GLORIA *looks around.)*
GLORIA.   Don't reckon this.
NATTRESS.   Silly.
GLORIA.   Not silly.
NATTRESS.   All right. Not silly.
GLORIA.   Turned the bloody light out. Wasn't silly.
NATTRESS.   I thought — I didn't think — it would be —
GLORIA.   Spooked me.
NATTRESS.   Don't like that word.
GLORIA.   It is!
NATTRESS.   Creepy. The English word is creepy.
GLORIA.   Why d'you do it?
NATTRESS.   If you must know I turned it on. But it was already on. So I turned it off. By accident. *(He is carrying a small fan-heater which he puts on the floor and plugs in at the wall.* GLORIA *watches him.)* I enjoy the English language. I try to speak it. And it is no longer very easy to speak. They say everyone speaks English, but that is not the case. Everyone speaks American. It is actually an effort to use words of purely English origin.
GLORIA.   Couldn't care.
NATTRESS.   You probably don't.
GLORIA.   I definitely don't. *(He switches on the heater.)*
NATTRESS.   It's quite warm really. *(He stretches out his hands.)*
GLORIA.   **Right on.**
NATTRESS.   These old walls are over five feet thick.
GLORIA.   **Uptight.**

NATTRESS.   Portland stone, brought here by sailing barges in the eighteenth century.

GLORIA.   **Ham — bur — ger.**

NATTRESS.   Very funny.

GLORIA.   I like American.

NATTRESS.   Please yourself.

GLORIA.   Ta. Ta very much. *(With inspiration.)* I mean **ta a million!** *(She giggles. Pause.)*

NATTRESS.   Do you want a seat?

GLORIA.   No.

NATTRESS.   Oh, go on, have a seat.

GLORIA.   I don't want a seat.

NATTRESS.   For a minute.

GLORIA.   What for? *(He looks at her, shrugs.)* Your neck's gone red.

NATTRESS.   Has it?

GLORIA.   Rash, is it? *(Pause.)*

NATTRESS.   I love this building. I actually love it very much . . . *(Pause.)*

GLORIA.   Still red. *(Pause.)*

NATTRESS.   You are going to make love, aren't you?

GLORIA.   Redder.

NATTRESS.   Gloria.

GLORIA.   **Very hot.**

NATTRESS.   Shall we? Please? *(She looks round, walks a few steps, stops.)*

GLORIA.   I think it is a filthy, smelly, rat-infested dump. *(Pause.)*

NATTRESS.   It is. It is. I admit that. But I quite like it. I like it a lot. *(Pause.)* I just do.

GLORIA *(with a shrug.)*   Well, if you like it . . .

NATTRESS.   It's the contrast I suppose, between the — the shabbiness and the —

GLORIA.   Okay, Fine. *(Pause.)*

NATTRESS.   I wonder if you sleep with many men?

GLORIA.   You do, do you?

NATTRESS.   Yes, I wonder.

GLORIA.   Ah. *(Pause.)*

NATTRESS.   This has got a preservation order on it. That shows you how historical it is. I love that. I love to think of the people who have been in here before us —

GLORIA.   Before me.

NATTRESS.   I meant —

GLORIA.   Before me. *(Pause.)* You meant. *(Pause.)* Where would you like to do it? *(Pause.)* Where? *(Pause.)* I take it you do have a special spot?

NATTRESS.   You are spoiling it for me.

GLORIA.   Sorry.

NATTRESS.   I would like this to be —

GLORIA.   Didn't mean to.

NATTRESS.   Would you try to make this more particular? Please? It is most particular for me.

GLORIA.   Okay.

NATTRESS.   By being a bit less casual?

GLORIA.   Yes. *(Pause. She turns away, walks a bit, turns back.)* **I love you.**

NATTRESS.   I didn't mean that — shit.

GLORIA.   **Amer — i — can!**

NATTRESS.   I didn't mean pretend. I do not want you to pretend. Not that pretence. I mean pretend — not to enjoy it. *(She stares at him.)* Say 'It's filthy in here.' 'It's too dirty.' Things like that. *(Pause. She gapes at him.)* It is dirty, after all. You said so yourself.

GLORIA.   Oh, God, Norman. *(Pause.)* Oh, **God.** *(He shrugs. She walks over to him, kisses him. Suddenly the light falters and goes out.)* **Nor — man!**

NATTRESS.   Only the light.

GLORIA.   For Christ's sake —

NATTRESS.   Bulb gone.

GLORIA.   Fuck it, get a light!

NATTRESS.   Just a bloody bulb gone.

GLORIA.   I don't care, will you get a fucking light!

NATTRESS.   Relax. Just keep still and relax.

GLORIA.   **Get me out of here!**

NATTRESS.   It is absolutely safe —

GLORIA.   **Touched something!**

NATTRESS.   It's only —

GLORIA.   **Will you get me out!**

NATTRESS.   I'll take you out. Just hang on, I'll take you out — *(He strikes a match.)* How's that?

GLORIA.   I want to go out. I want to go out.

NATTRESS.   It's absolutely safe — you only —

GLORIA.   I want **you** to take **me out**.

NATTRESS.   All right. I'll take you out.

He leads her out of the building. The light falters, comes on again. FINNEY appears behind the sacks. The coughing comes from off again, and the SPECTRE appears.

SPECTRE.   Where was I? *(He has a fit of spluttering.)* Where was I?

FINNEY.   Hilary.

SPECTRE.   Started work here 1st September 1922.

FINNEY.   Want to know if —

SPECTRE.   **Bloody hell!**

FINNEY.   Because I —

SPECTRE.   **Silly fucker's coming back!**

FINNEY.   Ought to — when she — when I — *(The SPECTRE is shuffling out again.)* **It's useless if we don't act decently.**

The SPECTRE goes out. Sound of a door slamming. FINNEY remains standing, then reluctantly goes back behind the sacks. Pause. NATTRESS reappears, carrying two cans of petrol. He stops.

NATTRESS.   Hello. These lights. These daft bloody lights. *(He looks up at the ceiling for a moment, puzzled. Then he puts the cans down. Pause as he looks down the warehouse hall.)* I am going to regret this. I shall never properly get over this. *(Pause.)* When you think what they will put up in its place. When you think of modern architects. Some glass house for kids to kick the windows in. Some boil festering on the landscape. *(Pause.)* When this could have stood for centuries. *(Pause, then he unscrews a can and starts sprinkling petrol about.)* Nelson came here. Almost certainly came here. For naval stores before the Battle of Trafalgar. One-eyed little genius kicking bits of rope with his buckled high-heeled shoes. *(He stops.)* Choosing his cannon-balls, I expect. *(Pause.)* Might have fixed to rendezvous with Lady Hamilton. Screwed her on a load of sacks. They were like that, uninhibited. *(He carries on sprinkling.)* And the Blitz, of course. Survived the Blitz. Takes more than bombs to knock down all that history. Takes a communist government. *(He throws the can aside. Reaches for his matches, strikes one.)*

FINNEY.   **There's someone here!** *(He pops up nervously.)*

NATTRESS *(hand in his pocket).*   **Got a gun!**

FINNEY.   Sorry, I was —

NATTRESS.   **Gun! Gun!**

FINNEY.   Afraid you'd —

NATTRESS.   This is private property!

FINNEY.   Yes, I was —

NATTRESS.   Right to shoot you! Got the right!

FINNEY.   Yes, sorry.

NATTRESS.   Got a heart condition. Not to have shocks.

FINNEY.   Oh, I am —

NATTRESS.   Doctor says I can't have shocks. *(Pause. They stare at each other.)* **Killer!**

FINNEY.   Sit down. *(Pause.)* I think you ought to sit. *(*NATTRESS *sits on the sacks. Pause.)*

NATTRESS.   Bit past it, aren't you? For a squatter? Are you squatting?

FINNEY.   I think so, yes.

NATTRESS.   I own this place.

FINNEY.   Yes.

NATTRESS.   **Well, then!** *(Pause.)*

FINNEY.   I am Finney. The Beast of Godalming. *(Long pause.)*

NATTRESS.   True or false?

FINNEY.   True. *(Pause.* NATTRESS *is rivetted.)*

NATTRESS.   Swear.

FINNEY.   I swear.

NATTRESS.   No. Say 'I swear it.' Not just 'I swear'.

FINNEY.   I swear it.

NATTRESS.   **Jesus Christ!** *(He gets up. Pause. He walks a little, goes back to* FINNEY, *gazes at his face, then he turns and suddenly gives the can a flying kick.)* Put me in a fucking spot! *(Pause. He thinks for some time.)* Finney. Are you normal?

FINNEY.   I don't think so.

NATTRESS.   I mean of course you're not normal, but are you roughly normal? Are you intelligent?

FINNEY.   Yes.

NATTRESS.   You understand plain English.

FINNEY.   Yes.

NATTRESS.   Well, what do you think these cans are for?

FINNEY.   Arson. *(Pause. He walks a little, turns again.)*

NATTRESS.   Finney, I am a bankrupt man. And I must have the insurance.
(Pause.) My father left me this place. This and a factory near Tooting. But
you **cannot run a business in this country any more.** *(Pause.)* Because it is a
workers' state. Behind our backs they've introduced a workers' state.
(Pause.) Well, they are not taking my property! *(Pause. He goes to*
FINNEY.*)* Follow me, do you? Or am I going too quick for you? *(Pause.)* I
am taking the insurance money and I am putting it in a country that respects
it. Someone has got to get this country right and that may well mean burning
it. **Scorched earth.** If England has to be a desert, whose fault is that? *(Pause.)*
Am I going too quick for you?

FINNEY.   This is an eighteenth century —

NATTRESS.   They knew how to build. *(Pause.)*

FINNEY.   No, I mean —

NATTRESS.   I know what you mean! *(Pause.)*

FINNEY.   They are forcing you to destroy England's heritage. *(*NATTRESS
looks at FINNEY *with a peculiar stare.)* They are forcing you to acts which
you are actually ashamed of. *(Pause.)* That is how we are now, isn't it? In a
madhouse?

NATTRESS.   Barbarians. I call this the second coming of the Barbarians.
(Pause.) It's all right. I never had a gun.

FINNEY.   I killed my kids.

NATTRESS.   So you did.

FINNEY.   To save them.

NATTRESS *(with a strange look.)*   Oh, yes . . .

FINNEY.   From socialism.

NATTRESS.   Ah . . .

FINNEY.   Like you are having to destroy this building. All because —

NATTRESS.   Driven to it.

FINNEY.   Yes. *(Pause.)* I'll do it.

NATTRESS.   What?

FINNEY.   Give us the matches.

NATTRESS.   Well, I — *(Pause. He thinks about it, then hands them over.)*
Would have hurt me. *(Pause.)* Would have done. *(Pause.)* Best open the
windows. For a draught. *(*FINNEY *nods.)* I'm in your debt. I call you a
patriot. If that does not embarrass you. You are a patriot.

FINNEY.   Take the cans out with me, shall I?

NATTRESS.   If you would.

FINNEY.   Insurance people —

NATTRESS.   Mad about cans.

FINNEY.   Quite. *(Pause. Then* NATTRESS *shakes his hand and turns to go
out. He stops near the exit.)*

NATTRESS.   There is a park up there. Above the docks. Certain caring
people meet at midnight by the clock. Englishmen. *(Pause.)* Good night.

He goes out. FINNEY *watches him, then goes to the empty can and removes it
towards the door. He picks up the other, finds it full, unscrews it and begins
spreading it around. As he works over the floor area,* ERICA *appears, eating*

from a bag of chips. She watches him. HILARY *joins her. At last he takes out a match and is about to strike it.*

ERICA.   Forgot the winders. *(He looks up. Pause.)*
HILARY.   Oh dear, Finney. Oh dear, oh dear . . .
ERICA.   Got to have the winders for the draught.
HILARY.   Finney is in crisis.
ERICA *(catching sight of it)*.   Look at my fucking sleeping bag!
HILARY.   Finney is **one step beyond**.
ERICA *(wringing petrol out of her sleeping bag)*.   Fucked it! How can I sleep in that? Fucked it!
HILARY.   He wishes to immolate himself. He fancies a very private auto-da-fe.
ERICA.   **Fuck him!**
HILARY.   I think he wants to tell us something. **Pyrothechincal communication is mass murderer's response to guilt.**
ERICA.   He is a stupid bastard. Someone ought to lock him up.
HILARY *(offering her bag)*.   Chip? Why don't you have a chip?
FINNEY *(mumbling)*.   Got to fight the workers' state.
HILARY.   Chip?
FINNEY.   **Got to fight the workers' state! Isn't anybody listening!** *(Pause.)*
ERICA.   What? What did he say?
FINNEY.   See, you're blind. All blind.
ERICA *(to* HILARY *)*.   Have you seen a workers' state? *(She pretends to look low.)* Can't see no workers' state.
HILARY.   Mind you, we're not actually looking for one . . .
FINNEY.   I have got to burn this building down.
HILARY.   Oh, why?
FINNEY.   I promised.
HILARY.   Ah, you promised.
FINNEY.   **Stop trying to make out I am mad**.
HILARY.   There's nothing intrinsically wrong with setting fire to things. Only when you happen to be living in them.
FINNEY.   We've got no right. The owner wants to burn it down.
HILARY.   **Nattress?**
FINNEY.   He needs the money.
HILARY.   **Nattress?** You've met **Nattress?**
FINNEY.   Yes, just now.
HILARY.   He's still alive . . .
FINNEY.   Heart troubles him. Can't be shocked. *(Pause.)* So let's leave, please.
ERICA.   **Certainly not.** *(Pause.)*
FINNEY.   I gave my word.
ERICA.   **No.**
FINNEY.   Look, you are being **unpatriotic!**

They look at him, then at each other. FINNEY *lets the matches fall to the floor. His head drops forward. After a few seconds he goes and collapses wearily on the sacks. Pause.*

ERICA.   They're wet. *(Pause.)* Finney. *(Pause.)* The sacks are wet.

Pause. Then HILARY *goes to him. He puts his arms round her waist, hugs her.* HILARY *looks at* ERICA. *Slow fade.*

Scene Six

The grounds of the devastated isolation hospital in Sussex. RUTKIN *is breaking up wood and tossing it on a fire. He picks up a fragment of the board which has 'Hospital' inscribed on it and proceeds to hack it with an axe. As he works a figure appears right, watching him silently. He is bare-headed, wears a long straggling raincoat and carries a plastic carrier bag, bulging with items. It is* FLUX. *He watches for some time, unobserved.*

FLUX.   Tell ye' fortoon. *(*RUTKIN *turns, looks at him, goes back.)* Pisces are, ye? Oot of interest. *(Pause.* RUTKIN *ignores him.)* Got a Pisces look about ye. *(Pause.)* Noo very friendly.

RUTKIN.   Got to be friendly, have I? New law says I got to be friendly?

FLUX.   I'm throo wi' the law, my friend.

RUTKIN.   I'm not your friend. *(Pause.)*

FLUX.   Figure o' speech. *(Long pause.* RUTKIN *tosses wood about.)* Lot o' fellars wuld gi' up wi' yoo. *(Pause.)* But I'm perseverin'. *(He puts the bag down, rummages in it, pulls out a pack of tarot cards.)* Take a card. *(He advances towards* RUTKIN, *fanning them.)* Any card. *(*RUTKIN *ignores him.)* Woon't bite ye.

RUTKIN.   Shouldn't be in here, grandad.

FLUX.   Okay, I took it for ye. It's the Hanged Man.

RUTKIN.   I'm authorized to report you to the police.

FLUX *(looking at the card).*   It's all right, it's upside doon. Reverse the message. It's a good one. Looked bad at first, then looked better.

RUTKIN.   **Grandad, are you deaf!** *(Pause.* FLUX *puts the cards away in his pocket, then bends down and takes a small plastic identity card out of his bag. He shows it to* RUTKIN.*)* Why didn't yer say so?

FLUX.   You are a pathetic man.

RUTKIN *(with a shrug).*   Okay.

FLUX.   You are a creepin' thing.

RUTKIN.   What can I do for yer?

FLUX.   Two inches o' plastic an' yoo are minus arms an' legs. Yoo are a wet fish on its belly.

RUTKIN.   Don't have to insult me. Didn't know you were a copper.

FLUX.   Ye knoo I was a man.

RUTKIN.   I thought you were a tramp, all right? *(Long pause.* FLUX *looks at him.)* What is this, anyway? We've had fire inspectors down. It was arson.

FLUX.   Gi' us yer name, lad.

RUTKIN.   Rutkin.

FLUX.   Well, look, Rutkin. I have information that a gel has been here.

RUTKIN.   Been where?

FLUX.   Ye're very cheeky for a flat fish, son.

RUTKIN.   Trying to be helpful.

FLUX.   I doubt that.

RUTKIN.   Asked a simple quest—

FLUX.   **Lookin' for a young gel, man!** *(Pause.* RUTKIN *gazes at him incredulously.)*

RUTKIN.   Show us that card again, would yer?

FLUX.   I came from Glasgow. My scalp is a braille map of hammer dents and bottle scars.

RUTKIN.   Could I?

FLUX.   On my head a blind man reads the history of a subspecies called Humanity. I have stood between the shit and the sugar. I have seen the ignorant carve the jawbones from the semi-educated and the savage kick the eyeballs from the sockets of the daft.

RUTKIN.   The card. I'd like another butchers at the card. *(He holds out his hand.)*

FLUX.   I had a wife and daughter. I came to London for the atmosphere.

RUTKIN.   Show us.

FLUX.   **I lost them both!** *(Pause, then he flicks the card into the fire.)* I ha' finished wi' policing.

RUTKIN.   Or did it finish with you?

FLUX.   They have dispensed wi' my services. In any case I was only eight months off pension. Now I am scouring the borders of the motorway.

RUTKIN.   Lone Ranger, eh?

FLUX.   She called me here. She is dark-haired an' beautiful.

RUTKIN.   All girls are beautiful. To their fathers. How beautiful?

FLUX.   Either ye knoo a woman's beautiful or ye doon't. I can't talk about borderline cases, where the beautiful sheers off into the pretty or the ugly into the passable. She was beautiful.

RUTKIN.   I haven't seen one.

FLUX.   Christ, wha' does a woman have to do to please ye!

RUTKIN.   I haven't seen her!

FLUX.   **She was here!** *(Pause.)*

RUTKIN.   Well, that's a sticky one. Because the only women I've seen here I wouldn't personally call beautiful.

FLUX.   Then ye're a fool. Or has she been in an accident.

RUTKIN.   Maybe I got no taste. I never thought my old woman was up to much. On the other hand I do think Raquel Welch is beautiful. Then look at Rubens. He thought great fat arses —

FLUX.   **Where has she gone?** *(Pause.)*

RUTKIN.   They got in a car. They had a bashed-up crate of a car.

FLUX.   Did ye follow 'em?

RUTKIN.   Why should I?

FLUX.   Ye shoold have followed 'em! Was she kidnapped? How did they treat her?

RUTKIN.   Kidnapped?

FLUX.   **Have you got the number?**

RUTKIN.   Didn't think of it —

FLUX.   **Jesus Christ!** *(Pause. He goes and sits, looking away, head in his hands.* RUTKIN *goes over to him. Pause.)*

RUTKIN.   Can't yer find a message in the cards?

FLUX.   They woon't talk to me. I am no a vessel for the aether.

RUTKIN.   Couldn't reach yer here in any case. Black air stops it. Thought it would clear when this place went. But kids have still got acne. Spuds still tasteless. Pus on the toadstools just the same. *(Pause.)*

FLUX.   I have no hope for the world. I have seen things on the pavement that made police dogs turn away. *(Pause.)* We have need of a reconciler, Rutkin. And I think his name is **God**. *(Suddenly there is a loud rush of wind which almost knocks RUTKIN over.)*

RUTKIN.   **Fuck!**

FLUX *(struggling up).*   **It's a sign! it is a sign!**

RUTKIN.   Can't stand up straight — bloody hell!

FLUX *(staggering to the fire).*   And there was a great wind, and a fire, and **the Lord spake!**

RUTKIN.   What — what —

FLUX.   **The sign! The sign!** *(He points to the fire.)* Where the smoke is blowing! What's over there?

RUTKIN.   The Green Man.

FLUX.   **Further!**

RUTKIN.   Crawley!

FLUX.   **Further!**

RUTKIN.   London, of course.

FLUX.   Then that's the place! *(He grabs up his bag, spilling it as he hurried off.)*

RUTKIN.   Fergot yer —

The wind stops. Sound of heavy rain. RUTKIN pulls up his jacket over his head. Slow fade.

Scene Seven

The park at midday. ERICA and HILARY are seated on the bench. Pause.

ERICA.   All right. You start.

HILARY.   Right. I want to talk about Finney.

ERICA.   Good. Because I want to talk about Finney too. *(Pause.)*

HILARY.   Right. *(Pause.)* I wonder if you'd start. *(Pause.)*

ERICA.   I think he's **mad**. *(Pause.)* For a start. *(Pause.)* But I'm not bothered by that.

HILARY.   Nope.

ERICA.   I don't think he's gonna murder us.

HILARY.   Me neither.

ERICA.   But I don't think I can stick his views. He gets up my nose.

HILARY.   All right.

ERICA.   I don't think we should be lumbered with a bloke who's got those views.

HILARY.   Go on.

ERICA.   That's all.

HILARY.   That's all.

ERICA.   Had me say.

HILARY.   Right.

ERICA.   Now you. *(Long pause.)*

HILARY.   Last night Finney got into my sleeping bag. *(Pause.)* All right? *(Pause.)* I felt this body and I thought there is only one person this can be. I thought I could stop this. At any moment I could stop it. But I didn't. *(Pause.)* I didn't actually enjoy it. *(Pause.)* Well, it was all right but nothing very special. I could have done without it but I didn't. All right? *(Pause.)* And of course he didn't take precautions. And I did think this might make me pregnant. The thought was there. Objective and transparent. I felt to resist the possibility would be to initiate a set of choices and I had already decided not to lumber myself with preferences. The world is hostile to preferences. It nullifies them. We discussed that, didn't we? And anyway he was crying. I can't stick an adult crying. I'd do anything to stop it. *(Pause.)* Finished. *(Pause.)*

ERICA.   Why don't you just call it sex?

HILARY.   What?

ERICA.   Sex. Just call it sex.

HILARY.   Oh, dear —

ERICA.   I'm not jealous but I wonder why you just can't say it's sex.

HILARY.   Oh dear, oh dear . . .

ERICA.   All this **nullifying possibilities.** Just call it **sex.**

HILARY.   I thought this might —

ERICA.   Don't insult me.

HILARY.   If you're jealous will you say so —

ERICA.   **Don't insult me.** *(Pause.)* It is his views I cannot stick. I don't think you can ignore what people think. *(Pause.)* I'm sorry but I think it matters.

HILARY.   The world is a constant image no matter how you shake the bits. It is kaleidescopic. You shake it and the coloured bits move but the ingredients are the same. That is why we reject politics.

ERICA.   I got that.

HILARY.   So what Finney thinks does not matter.

ERICA.   No. *(Pause.)* At least I thought it didn't but I'm not sure.

ERICA.   Are you in love with Finney?

ERICA.   **Oh, fuck!**

HILARY.   If he prefers me it is only because of some meaningless aesthetic.

ERICA.   **I don't want fucking Finney! That's not it!** *(Pause.)* I'm thinking, that's all. *(Pause.)* Whether it matters. What he thinks. That's all. *(Pause.)* I have ter think. *(Pause.)* Don't I? **I have ter think.**

The lights fade down for night. They go out as the next scene opens.

Scene Eight

Night time in the park. A youth enters, waving a pair of men's trousers. He dances about, calling to someone offstage.

HAMMICK.   What am I bid! What am I bid! One pair Terylene —*(He stops, examines the label.)* sorry — Terylene and cotton — gents trousers — slightly shiny on the bum — otherwise in good condition — *(He sniffs at the crutch.)* whoah! Could do wiv a clean — few stains around the zip — but — *(He rushes offstage as* CROYDON, *without his trousers, comes in.)*

CROYDON.   **Come here!** Oi, come on, **Come here!** *(Pause. he folds his arms.)* I'm not chasin' yer. When you've grown up I'll have 'em back. When you're ready. *(*HAMMICK *reappears on tiptoe. Holding the trousers in front of him.)*

HAMMICK.   Semen stains around the arse — definite evidence of certain — shall we say **malpractices?**

CROYDON.   I'm not chasing yer.

HAMMICK.   He's not chasin' me.

CROYDON.   You enjoy yerself and then I'll have 'em back, thank you.

HAMMICK.   He thanks me. He tells me to enjoy myself.

CROYDON.   When you're ready.

HAMMICK *(holding them up for examination).*   I don't exactly **like** your trousers. I mean I think you've got **horrible** taste, Don . . . I wouldn't inflict these trousers on a dosser.

CROYDON.   Have you finished?

HAMMICK.   No. *(He looks around, holding them aloft.)* I will take — for this **tasteless** pair of trousers — I will take — not ten — not even five — no, not even **two** — but —*(The clock begins chiming midnight.* CROYDON *charges at* HAMMICK *.)*

CROYDON.   **Give 'em to us!**

HAMMICK *dashes off, pursued by* CROYDON. *The clock is finishing its chimes as* NATTRESS, *in overcoat and trilby, appears. He looks out over the lights of London.*

NATTRESS.   London . . . you old carcass . . . Bombay will be the hub of the world before you are again . . .

HAMMICK *crashes in, brought down by* CROYDON *almost at* NATTRESS' *feet. He yells breathlessly, rolls onto his back giggling as* CROYDON *recovers his trousers.*

CROYDON.   Norman. *(He climbs into them.)* Got here all right, then. *(He zips them up.)* That's a view, ain't it?

NATTRESS.   Might be another chap along tonight.

CROYDON *(adjusting himself).*   Don't spread the net too wide.

NATTRESS *(looking at* HAMMICK *).*   Don't **you.**

CROYDON.   Know what I'm doing. *(He looks at* HAMMICK *).* Get up, Willy. *(Pause.)* **Willy, get up.** *(*HAMMICK *climbs to his feet, brushing grass off his clothes.)* This is Mr Nattress.

HAMMICK *(extending a hand).*   Evening. *(*NATTRESS *doesn't shake hands.)*

CROYDON.   Right. Get over there. Watch out. *(As* HAMMICK *goes off,* BRILLIANT *comes in.)*

BRILLIANT.   Sorry I'm late. Kid's got tonsilitis.

HAMMICK *(coming in).*   **Geezer wanderin'!**

CROYDON *(to* NATTRESS*).*   Is this your bloke?

HAMMICK.   Wha' shall I do?

NATTRESS.   Finney. Call him Finney.

HAMMICK *(going off).* **Finney ... Finney is it ... ?**

CROYDON.   I wish we could get on with this.

NATTRESS.   Got all night before us.

BRILLIANT.   Not the whole night, I'm afraid. Not for me.

CROYDON.   Tonsils first, eh Brian? England last.

BRILLIANT.   You should see 'em.

CROYDON.   I would rather not, thank you. *(*FINNEY *appears, nervously at the edge of the stage.)*

FINNEY.   Mr Nattress? *(He comes nearer.)* Sorry about the fire.

NATTRESS.   Slipped up, did you?

FINNEY.   I did it but there was a problem —

CROYDON.   Can we talk about these separate matters at another time? As we are short of time tonight. Because of Brian's domestic problems. Can we get on? *(They look at him.)* Thank you. *(Pause.)* I deem the moment has arrived to make the transition from **theory** into **practice**. *(Pause.)* **Relax, Brian.** *(Pause.)* We are steeped in theory now, but theory is like steam. It is useless if it just pours out the kettle. All it does is make the walls wet. But steam in a cylinder can shift a train of coal trucks.

NATTRESS.   Hear, hear.

CROYDON.   So, I propose the initiation of a little action. *(Pause. He walks a little way, taking in the lights.)* May I refer you to the view? All your ideas ought to be related to that view. *(Pause.)* Brian. What is stimulated in your head by it? *(Pause.* BRILLIANT *shrugs.)* Something, surely? **Come on.**

BRILLIANT.   The lights.

CROYDON.   The lights, yes ...

BRILLIANT.   **One switch.**

CROYDON.   I told you that three months ago. *(Pause.)* Norman? *(Pause.)*

NATTRESS.   The littleness.

CROYDON.   Interesting.

NATTRESS.   The fact that I can put my hand across it.

CROYDON.   Go on.

NATTRESS.   And blot it out.

CROYDON.   Go on.

NATTRESS.   The fact that it takes so little to obliterate so much.

CROYDON.   Switch theory. Yup. Keep going.

NATTRESS.   And ... *(Pause.)* And if you find the right nerves ... you can cut a limb off ... and the body never feels it ...

CROYDON.   Now yer talking.

NATTRESS.   That accupuncture, for example, says **one needle, one point** of a **single needle** in the right place and the whole body registers ...

CROYDON.   I like this. I know where he's going and I like it.

NATTRESS.   I am talking about the **Bank of England** ...

CROYDON.   Correct.

NATTRESS.   **The BBC** ...

CROYDON.   Spot on.

NATTRESS.   **10 Downing Street ...**
CROYDON.   He's got it. He has got it. Thank you, Norman.
NATTRESS.   The rest is just waiting. The Queen and the Duke, and the City
   of London, and the Archbishop of Canterbury, they are merely waiting.
   They will welcome us with open arms. Be sure of that. And the rest of —
CROYDON.   Thank you, Norman. Mr Finney, any points? *(Pause.)*
FINNEY.   They are ruining our country ...
CROYDON.   Yup. Anything more practical, though? *(Pause.)*
FINNEY.   The people are just sitting back ...
CROYDON.   Procedure, though? *(Pause.)*
FINNEY.   If we could get the people to —
CROYDON.   That's what we're doing. That's what we want.
BRILLIANT.   I just wonder if we're ready yet. Because — I can't stop long —
   perhaps we haven't picked the proper moment. The timing's the important
   thing.
CROYDON.   Perhaps Norman would answer that one. Norman?
NATTRESS.   I have shut my factory in Tooting. I have opened one in Spain.
   The workers won't work here and the West End is full of foreigners. **How
   much worse should it get?** *(*BRILLIANT *shrugs. There is a scream
   offstage.)*
HAMMICK.   **Got 'im! Got 'im!** *(*HAMMICK *appears kicking and dragging
   the form of* METHS.*)* Fuckin' snoopin'! Fuckin' sneakin' on us!
METHS.   I was not! I was not!
HAMMICK.   On his hands and fuckin' knees **listenin'!**
METHS.   **Help me! Help me!**
CROYDON.   Keep him quiet for fuck's —
METHS.   **Help me!**
HAMMICK.   Dirty ol' cunt was spyin'!
CROYDON.   **Shut him up!**
HAMMICK *(kicking him).*   Shut it!
METHS.   **Mur-der!**
HAMMICK *(mocking him).*   **Mur-der!**
BRILLIANT *(turning away).*   Bloody hell ... *(as* HAMMICK *kicks* METHS
   on the ground, NATTRESS *watches, while* FINNEY *is transfixed.)*
HAMMICK.   **Shut it! Shut it!**
METHS.   **Fas-cist bas-tards!**
HAMMICK.   **Get washed you filth!**
BRILLIANT *(some feet away).*   I think — I do think — can we —
METHS.   **Mos-ley shit!**
BRILLIANT.   Don, should we —
HAMMICK.   **Filth! Filth!**
BRILLIANT.   Don —
METHS.   **My eyes! My bleeding eyes!**
CROYDON.   All right, Willy ...
HAMMICK.   **Killing him! I'm killing him!**
FINNEY *(at the pitch of his voice).*   **St-op!**
BRILLIANT.   Off, lad —
FINNEY.   **St-op!**

CROYDON *(pulling* HAMMICK *away with* BRILLIANT*).*   **All right, I
    said.** *(They stand back.* METHS *is a heap on the ground.)*
METHS.   My eyes . . . you've . . . *(Pause.)* **Where's my eyes!** *(He crawls a
    little.)*You've . . . *(Pause.)* **Oh, my eyes!**
HAMMICK.   'When Irish eyes are smilin' . . . '
CROYDON.   **Shuddup.**
HAMMICK.   What's black and crashes into pianos?
CROYDON.   **Shuddup.**
HAMMICK.   Little Stevie Wonder.
METHS.   **Kill me!** *(Pause.)* I wanna die. *(Pause.)* **Will you please kill me?**
    (Pause.)
CROYDON.   You heard him.
BRILLIANT.   Blimey —
CROYDON.   **We heard him.** *(Pause.)*
NATTRESS.   It might be better. As it's gone so far.
METHS.   **Do it. Fuck you. Do it.**
CROYDON *(to* HAMMICK*).*   Quick. *(Pause, then* HAMMICK *bends to*
    METHS. FINNEY *covers his ears and eyes.* BRILLIANT *walks a few paces
    away.* HAMMICK *stands up.)* Now go home, Willy. Please. *(*HAMMICK
    goes out.) Listen everybody. This is Brian's patch. Brian will see to it.
BRILLIANT.   Oh, **fuck. Fuck. Fuck.**
CROYDON.   It is the time, you see Brian. Now is the time.
BRILLIANT.   **Fuck.**
CROYDON.   Shake hands with everybody. Then go home. *(*NATTRESS
    extends his hand. BRILLIANT *takes it, looks at* FINNEY, *who is quite still.)*
    And Mr Finney. *(As* FINNEY *doesn't move,* BRILLIANT *touches his hand
    quickly, then goes out. Pause.)* All right, Norman? *(*NATTRESS *nods, then
    indicates* FINNEY.*)* Got a first name, has he?*(*NATTRESS *shrugs.*
    CROYDON *goes to* FINNEY.*)* Well, Finney . . . *(Pause.* FINNEY *just
    looks down.)* We came here tonight and we were four — five — different
    people. But we go home one person. We go home united in that man's blood.
    (Pause.) Do you see that? How he has bound us together in our cause?
    (Pause.) We are shifting history. We are turning over the times and you can't
    do that without there being accidents. We aren't superhuman, we are only
    flesh. If flesh bleeds, whose fault is that? *(Pause.* FINNEY *kneels beside the
    form of* METHS.*)* I wouldn't look at it . . . *(*NATTRESS *wags his finger at*
    CROYDON. *Pause. Then* FINNEY *gets to his feet.)*
FINNEY.   I don't get it. *(Pause.)*
CROYDON.   What?
FINNEY.   What makes an old tramp into a socialist.
CROYDON.   Socialist?
FINNEY.   **Spying on us! Got to be a Socialist!**
CROYDON.   Yeah, obviously —
FINNEY.   What did socialism do for him? *(*CROYDON *lifts his hands in
    studied bewilderment.)* Don't get it. *(Pause.)* Don't get it.

Fade to black.

ACT TWO

Scene One

The vaults of the Bank of England. Two BEEFEATERS *are standing midstage. One with a pike, one holding a massive bunch of keys. Sound of marching feet. A patrol of* GUARDSMEN *enters, led by an* OFFICER *with a sword. They all wear red tunics and bearskins. They halt.*

FIRST BEEFEATER. Who comes here?
OFFICER. We come for the keys.
FIRST BEEFEATER. In whose authority?
OFFICER. Elizabeth the Second.
FIRST BEEFEATER. Who will guard them?
OFFICER. I will guard them. *(The* OFFICER *stamps forward.)*
FIRST BEEFEATER. How will you guard them?
OFFICER. With my life.

The BEEFEATER *presents the keys to the* OFFICER. *At the same moment the* SOLDIERS *present arms.*

SOLDIERS. **Elizabeth the Second! God bless her! God bless the realm!**

The OFFICER *marches backwards with the keys to stand in front of his men. The* BEEFEATERS *about turn, march off. The* OFFICER *and two of the* SOLDIERS *follow them with the keys. The two remaining* SOLDIERS *stand easy. Long pause.*

FIRST PRIVATE. What was I saying?
SECOND PRIVATE. Surplus profit.
FIRST PRIVATE. Oh, yeah. Surplus profit is the labour hours performed by the worker but not paid by the employer.
SECOND PRIVATE. Labour hours?
FIRST PRIVATE. Example. You work a ten hour day.
SECOND PRIVATE. Yeah.
FIRST PRIVATE. The employer only pays you for six.
SECOND PRIVATE. Why?
FIRST PRIVATE. His profit is made out of the remaining four.
SECOND PRIVATE. Lost me. *(Pause.)*
FIRST PRIVATE. Profit.
SECOND PRIVATE. Yeah.
FIRST PRIVATE. You know profit.

SECOND PRIVATE.   I know profit.

FIRST PRIVATE.   Comes from the workers.

SECOND PRIVATE.   Exploitation.

FIRST PRIVATE.   Correct. Surplus labour is the labour put into a product for which the worker is not paid. *(Pause.)* Fucking —

SEOND PRIVATE.   Question.

FIRST PRIVATE.   I told yer!

SECOND PRIVATE.   May I ask a question? *(Pause.)* Why does the worker let the employer get away with it? *(Pause.)* If he only gets paid from eight until two, why does he go on working until half past five?

FIRST PRIVATE.   It's a theory. They call it a theory. Karl Marx spent ages working on —

He is silent as FINNEY *appears. He stands about uncomfortably, looks offstage. At last he addresses first private.*

FINNEY.   Have I missed it? *(Pause.)* Have I missed the ceremony of the Keys? *(They ignore him. He takes out a card.)* I have a vistor's pass for the Ceremony of the Keys. *(As they continue to ignore him, he puts the card away again. He wanders a little more, then goes boldly up to the* SOLDIERS *again.)* The red tunics. Lie in every corner of the globe. Must be proud of England. Difficult I know, but wait. Call to all our soldiers soon. *(He looks at them. Pause.)*

FIRST PRIVATE.   **Fuck ... off**

FINNEY *is embarrassed. Sound of marching feet again as the* OFFICER *returns with his squad.* FINNEY *moves deftly out of the way and taking out a note pad, jots down details of the number of men. All the* SOLDIERS *march off, leaving him alone.*

FINNEY.   Ten Downing Street. One PC changed at two-hour intervals. One panda car on quarter hours. The BBC. Two uniformed staff on the door, changed at three hour intervals. Bank of England. Two Beefeaters, armed. Five soldiers, bayonets. *(As he reads this out,* ERICA *comes in, stands watching him.)*

ERICA.   Tower of London next?

FINNEY *(spinning round, stuffing the pad away).*   No right to follow me!

ERICA.   Got a thing about damp vaults?

FINNEY.   Spy.

ERICA.   Buy us an ice-cream.

FINNEY.   No right to spy! *(Pause. She goes up to him, as if confidentially.)*

ERICA.   Finney. The bank happens **Upstairs.** This is the tourist bit.

FINNEY.   Why are you following me?

ERICA *(shaking her head at him).*   You daft git. *(He turns and starts to go.)* Yer can't go yet. I got some news for yer. *(He stops.)* I bear a message of the utmost secrecy. *(Pause.)*

FINNEY.   What?

ERICA *(wandering, gazing at the roof).*   These ol' cellars, drippin, and crumblin' ... stinkin' of **English history** ... *(She looks at him.)* Not that fond of history myself ... *(Pause.)* When I was a kid I used to wonder if I was an offshoot of the aristocracy. The bastard line of some old English family. I thought I might have had an ancestor whose picture was hanging up in some big house. It used to matter to me. It really did. Wasn't that a compliment? That I should have been so keen to have a bit of their blood in me? Real fucking loyalty —

FINNEY.   I don't want to hear class hatred. *(He starts to go out.)*

ERICA.   I haven't told you the news yet! *(He stops.)* You do want the news, don't you? *(Pause.)* My grandad was killed at Gallipoli. My dad said it was a balls-up. Because of the lousy English officers.

FINNEY.   If you've got something to tell me will you —

ERICA.   **Finney, why don't you talk to me!** *(He looks at her.)* They got the British Empire going and silly buggers like my grandad went and —

FINNEY.   Give me the message and —

ERICA.   **Why won't you talk to me!** *(Pause.)*

FINNEY.   I am not ashamed of England. *(Pause.)* I'm not ashamed of it.

ERICA.   Finney. There isn't any England any more. It didn't work and so they chucked it.

FINNEY.   Socialists — **Socialists — ruined — it!**

ERICA.   Got to see for yourself. Through the racket and the rattle. Feel it yourself.

FINNEY.   **Save our country. Save it. Only right.**

ERICA.   Where is it then?

FINNEY.   Where is it?

ERICA.   England. Where is it? Is this it? Traitor's Gate and Horseguards? Houses of Parliament? Is it? What are you doing here, Finney? Looking for History? I tell you, History's gone!

FINNEY.   Gone, has it? Where has it gone?

ERICA.   Up there! History's on the telephone fixing a deal with Düsseldorf! They have chucked England, Finney, England's dead. England's a mothy uniform with Nelson's blood on it and Tudor clubs for financiers to dip their pricks. *(He turns away in contempt.)* Got to talk about it, Finney. Got to talk. *(He turns to go.)* Hilary's pregnant. *(Pause.)* That's the news. *(He stops.)* She asked me to tell yer because she thought if she did it would have connotations of . . . you know . . . it could seem romantic . . . and it's not. *(Pause.)* She is gonna have it but it puts you under no obligations *(Pause.)* Now **I'll** go *(She walks out quickly.)*

FINNEY.   **She can't! Not in this — how can she!**

He starts to follow ERICA out. Stops. Spins round, strides back. Stops. Puts his hands to his head, remains thus for some seconds. There comes the sound of a tubercular cough, and the SPECTRE shuffles on stage. Stops before him. Pause. FINNEY takes his fingers from his eyes.

FINNEY.   Don't say you were a bloody beefeater . . .

SPECTRE.   Cherish it, Finney.

FINNEY.   What?

SPECTRE.   The kiddie. Rejoice.

FINNEY.   **Rejoice?** *(Pause.)*

SPECTRE.   I said —

FINNEY.   When the world's like this — **Rejoice?**

SPECTRE.   You like babies.

FINNEY.   **I'm not thinking of myself.**

SPECTRE.   Try it. A man who can't think of his own interests can't help other people's.

FINNEY.   A kid can't hope to —

SPECTRE.   Your **own** feelings, Finney.

FINNEY.   What chance has it —

SPECTRE.   **Don't hold it back.** *(*FINNEY *clasps his hands to his head.)* **Don't hold it back!**

FINNEY.   The world — the world —

SPECTRE.   **Fuck the world!**

FINNEY.   **All right, I want it!**

SPECTRE.   You're glad?

FINNEY.   **I'm glad!**

SPECTRE.   You see?

FINNEY.   **I'm glad, I'm glad, I'm bloody glad!**

SPECTRE.   Yer see?

FINNEY.   **Damn bloody glad!**

SPECTRE.   All right, yer see?

FINNEY.   **Only a madman would be glad!** *(Pause.* SPECTRE *looks at him.)*

SPECTRE.   I was in the First World War. In a gully in Gallipoli. Our generals never set foot on the beach. They watched us dying through binoculars. Sitting on yachts with iced cocktails in their hands, while we were sucking pebbles and our bowels gushed with dysentry. The bloke beside me put the muzzle of his rifle in his mouth. I watched him ease his boot off, put his big toe in the trigger. 'Don't be fucking mad,' I said. He turned to me. He had such a cocky grin across his face. 'Who's fucking mad,' he said. **Bang.** *(Pause.)* Got to be mad to live, Finney . . . *(*FINNEY *doesn't reply.* SPECTRE *shuffles out. As he does so, sound of marching feet, and two* BEEFEATERS *enter.)*

FIRST BEEFEATER.   I'm afraid you have missed the ceremony of the keys.

SECOND BEEFEATER.   Your next opportunity will come at half past three.

FIRST BEEFEATER.   Worth hanging about for.

SECOND BEEFEATER.   Kiddies love it.

FIRST BEEFEATER.   The chants. They love the chants.

SECOND BEEFEATER.   Exactly as recited in the eighteenth century. *(They start to march off.)*

FINNEY.   I'll bring her . . . *(Suddenly he calls after them.)* **What's up there?** *(He points to the roof. Pause.)*

FIRST BEEFEATER.   Typists.

SECOND BEEFEATER.   Clerks and typists. Wih their hands in one another's knickers.

They go out. Fade to black.

Scene Two

The park at midday. HILARY *stands midstage.* ERICA *is on the bench.* FINNEY *some distance away.*

HILARY.   You see I was afraid of this. *(She looks at* ERICA *.)* Wasn't I?
*(*ERICA *looks down.)* I saw it looming in the distance. I saw that Finney's
mastery of **my** body would lead to the complete enslavement of **his** mind.
But there is always this yawning gulf between what you know and what you
do about it. And there are going to be occasions when your resistance will be
low. Such as two in the morning when groping fingers steal across your bed.
And after all, why shouldn't you? Aren't I entitled to a flicker of **relief**?
(Pause.) Dad bought us a house. A big house with two lavatories and half-
louvred doors that swung and hit you like the Crazy Horse Saloon. It was a
posh street but bang in the middle was this comprehensive. I didn't go to the
comprehensive. I went to the convent. I had this brown school uniform. I
ddidn't know it at the time, but I looked good. As far as some men are
concerned I have never looked that good since. And there was this particular
kid who shouted at me, because they were always coming out as I was going
in. I put up with it until one day instead of calling me a snob he asked me did I
want a fuck. Which made his fan club fall about. And I knew from then on it
would become the standard greeting, and as I was only fifteen and he was
younger it would be a long time to put up with it. And certain to get dirtier. So
the next night when he made this rhetorical suggestion I said yes.
ERICA.   I have heard this, Hilary —
HILARY.   **I am telling this story because people are so sticky!** *(Pause.*
ERICA *shrugs.* HILARY *goes and sits on the bench.)* It happened once or
twice. Then when I said get lost the acned creature cut his wrists. *(Pause.)*
ERICA.   Poor ol' Hilary.
HILARY.   I am saying —
ERICA.   I know what you're saying, darling —
HILARY.   No, I don't think you do know. Because it is not within the scope of
your experience.
ERICA.   Say something, Finney! defend your bloody little passion! *(Pause.*
FINNEY *looks up.)*
FINNEY.   I'm sorry, I —
ERICA.   That's wrong, sweetheart. *(Pause.)* Isn't it? *(Pause.)* Wrong tack.
(Pause.)
FINNEY.   I want the child. I want to be involved with it. And you.
ERICA.   But not necessarily in that order.
FINNEY.   I am the father and I have a **right**. *(Pause.)* I think.
HILARY.   I am hyper-fertile. You were adequate. The rest is sentiment.
FINNEY.   That isn't **fair.**
ERICA.   Oh God, Finney . . .
FINNEY *(turning to her).* Is it?
ERICA.   Why don't you say it?
HILARY.   What?
ERICA.   He fancies the shit out of you! *(Pause.* FINNEY *just stands there.)*
He can't, yer see . . . *(Pause.)* Can you? *(*FINNEY *seems to struggle to
speak. Suddenly he turns and hurries out.* ERICA *follows him to the edge of
the stage and calls after him.)* **Where is it today? The TUC?** *(Pause. She
comes slowly back.* HILARY *is standing on the bench looking over
London.)*

HILARY.   That view says to me — roll on Nagasaki . . .   *(Pause.)*

ERICA.   I don't think I get on with you any more. *(Pause.)* I think it's because you are so beautiful I went for you in the first place.

HILARY.   All you had in the world was a railway-warrant from a remand home. You were cadging cannabis on Waterloo . . .

ERICA.   I thought you had style. I wanted to get close to you. I even managed to get my periods to coincide with yours. That's how much I thought of you. *(Pause.)* I still think you have style, but I don't think it matters any more. *(Pause.)* Sorry. *(Long pause.)* Blimey, **don't you care!** *(Pause, then* HILARY *gets down from the bench and comes over to her, removing a necklace. She stands in front of* ERICA.*)*

HILARY.   You don't like jewellery, do you?

ERICA.   Never had any.

HILARY *places the necklace on* ERICA's *neck. As she does so,* FLUX *appears, holding his bag. He goes naturally to the bench and stands on it, holding the bag in front of him. He addresses the girls, but only as part of a vaster audience.* HILARY *steps back at last, looks at* ERICA . . .

FLUX.   I'll tell ye a secret. I'll tell ye a secret which is both a secret and noo a secret. It is noo a secret because I have told so many people. There are so many people party to it, it is technically noo a proper secret. On the other hand, it is tucked into a corner of their heads, or maybe a corner of their hearts and they do noo wanna hear it. It makes them squirm and shift their feet. And when I tell ye, ye'll squirm and act like I have uncovered yer pudenda. It is that embarrassin'. So get ready, and the timid among ye' hide yer heads. *(Pause.)* Are ye ready? All right then. *(Pause.)* **Ye are guid.** *(Pause. He looks as if from face to face.)*

ERICA.   Oh, fuck . . .

FLUX.   I was married to a prostitute. I ha' noo shame in sayin' tha'. She had a body an' it was the body that I married, so I was a prostitute mysel'. She was a dancer, an' I laid eyes on her, an' my body trembled .

ERICA.   **Get on wiv it!**

FLUX.   An' I went back, an' I went back. I sat in the darkness wi' other hungry men an' watched her. I watched her wi' my body. I did na watch her wi' my mind.

ERICA.   **Dirty ol' bastard!**

FLUX.   An' while I was degraded by her, she was degraded by me. I was emptyin' my bowels on that woman, an' she was emptying her bowels on me.

ERICA *(mock expression of disgust).* **Fucking hell . . .**

FLUX.   It was a filthy trading of excreta —

ERICA *(laughing).* **Children play in here, grandad!**

FLUX.   A squalid, genital deal. So how could I satisfy this woman, when I had prevailed upon her to marry me, to share my bed? How could I satisfy the insatiable, eat the inedible, swallow the unswallowable —

ERICA.   **Get on wiv it!**

FLUX.   I am gettin' on with it. *(Pause.)* I brought her to my home, an' I brought her garments —

ERICA.   **Gar-ments?**

FLUX.   An' I did all that I culd, but it was filling the bottomless pit because **there was noo guid in it!** I had shut the **guid** from me. I had kept my **guid** a secret. *(Pause. He looks around.)*
ERICA.   I'm going.
HILARY.   Why?
ERICA.   Can't stick him. *(Pause.)*
HILARY.   Don't go yet.
ERICA.   Why not?

Pause. HILARY *shrugs, looks at her a moment, then kisses her. Pause. Then* ERICA *goes out,* HILARY *watching her. She keeps her back to* FLUX *as she watches* ERICA *disappear across the park.*

FLUX.   Had I set free my **guid**, had I said to my **guid**, come forward **guid** and lead me! Then I would ha' known a different life. An' to all of ye out there, to all the people who are ashamed or frightened of their **guid** I say **let the guid speak!** *(He raises his arm over London.)* Because there is violence of man agin man in the pubs and alleys, an' man agin woman in brothels an' smart sitting-rooms, an' man agin employer in factories, an' poor agin the rich, all because they are timid of their **guid!** *(Pause. His hand shakes.* HILARY *turns to him.)*
HILARY.   Hello, Dad. *(He stares at her.)* Come on. Let's get shot of London . . .

Blackout.

Scene Three

A tube station. A large blank station sign. It is late at night. FINNEY *is waiting for a train. After some time, sound of a bucket and broom, whistling. A* STATIONMAN *appears, dumps his bucket, reaches into his pocket.*

STATIONMAN.   Lockin' up.
FINNEY.   Isn't there —
STATIONMAN.   No, guv. *(He removes a spraycan from his pocket and begins writing* 'LABOUR IS BOSSES' *across the sign.)* Not till tomorrer morning, guv. Four forty-four. I'm lockin' up, yer see. Kip down here if yer like. People used to in the war. Not that it was an orgy or nothing. Not like it would be today. Be sirens on and knickers off now, wouldn't it? *(He puts the lid back on the can, replaces it in his pocket.)* Help yerself to Fruit and Nut. That machine there's busted. Good enough for breakfast, if yer fancy it. *(He picks up the bucket and is about to move off.)*
FINNEY *(looking at the slogan).*   You mean 'Labour is the boss', don't you? *(Pause. The man stops.)* Can't be bosses. *(Pause.)* Can it?
STATIONMAN.   It says what's going on. That's what it says.
FINNEY.   Labour **are** the bosses —
STATIONMAN.   **It's going on!** *(Pause.)*
FINNEY.   Yes, I was only . . . *(Pause.)* Grammatical . . . *(Pause.)* That's all . . . *(The* STATIONMAN *starts to go, stops, comes back. As he talks, he emphasizes each word with his broom handle.)*

STATIONMAN.   Labour Government — is — the Bosses. *(He looks at* FINNEY *who doesn't respond.)* So-called Socialists — are in league with — Capitalists. *(*FINNEY *shrugs. Impatiently, the* STATIONMAN *thumps the sign again.)* Treacherous, fornicating, misnomered **Labour** government — is working in the interests of — Fucking International Capital! *(Pause.)* **Get it?** *(Pause.)*
FINNEY.   I have a child coming and I — *(Suddenly the lights falter and go off.)*
STATIONMAN.   Fuck. Some silly bugger's turned the lights out. **Oi!** *(He starts moving about. The bucket sounds.)* Find the emergency. Hold it. Along here somewhere. That's it. *(Nothing happens.)* **Fuck it!** All right if there was a bloody emergency, fuck it.
FINNEY.   **Hil-ary!**
STATIONMAN.   Eh?
FINNEY *(dashing about in the dark).* **Hil-ary!**
STATIONMAN.   Look, what is this! *(Sound of a falling bucket and broom.)*
FINNEY.   **My baby's dead!**

 Blackout.

Scene Four

A gymnasium. A vaulting horse, fixed cycle, ropes. Lying on his back in shorts, CROYDON, *attempting to raise a 24lb bar.* NATTRESS *comes in, wearing scarf and overcoat.*

NATTRESS.   Don.
CROYDON.   Ugh . . . Ugh . .
NATTRESS *(watching him).*   How I got my hernia.
CROYDON.   Ugh . . . Ugh . . .
NATTRESS.   Putting you off? *(He starts walking away.)* Might be putting you off, I suppose. *(With a massive heave,* CROYDON *raises the bar.* NATTRESS *looks back from the door.)* Oh, well done. *(He goes out. After a few seconds,* CROYDON *brings the bar down. He sits up. Pause.)*
CROYDON.   Had a bit of bad luck last night, then? *(Pause.)* Plus a high wind. *(He goes to the cycle and climbs on.)* Had the Conservation ladies round first thing. Great gnashing teeth across my desk. You might have found it sexy. Begging for more coppers round the docks. *(He pedals very quickly for ten seconds, stops.)* Said the place was built by Adam someone — did you know? *(He pedals again, stops.* NATTRESS *comes in wearing shorts.)*
NATTRESS.   Mister Adam.
CROYDON.   Could have been.
NATTRESS.   You're on my bike.
CROYDON *(getting off).* Assessors coming down today?
NATTRESS *(climbing on).*   Poking in the cinders. Treading on English history. *(He thinks for a moment, then starts cycling leisurely.* CROYDON *picks up a dumbell and starts raising it.)*
CROYDON.   Pity about the body. *(*NATTRESS *stops cycling.* CROYDON *goes on raising the dumbell.)*

NATTRESS. Come again.
CROYDON. Come again?
NATTRESS. Beg pardon.
CROYDON. Never heard you say that. **Come again**, slip of the elocution.
NATTRESS. Don.
CROYDON. Nasty one.
NATTRESS. **Please Don.** *(CROYDON stops exercising his arm.)*
CROYDON. They have found a body.
NATTRESS. Whose?
CROYDON. A lady. Judging by the pelvis. And a bit of necklace stuck to it. *(Pause. NATTRESS gets off the bike. He starts walking to the door, stops. He covers his face.)* Have a shower. *(Pause.)* Norman. *(Pause. Then NATTRESS takes his hands away, turns back to CROYDON.)*
NATTRESS. I had fifteen different women in that place . . .
CROYDON. Who needs Brighton?
NATTRESS. I have a thing about them. Women, I mean.
CROYDON. A lot of people do, boy.
NATTRESS. I mean a special thing. I mean I have got — worse — not better, with the passing years. I think it may be an illness. Or a condition.
CROYDON. Not to worry.
NATTRESS. Because of England. The state of England. Makes me think of them. *(CROYDON looks at him peculiarly.)* In places where there is a leader — Russia, say — or China — there is less interest in women. Under Churchill, I was not half so keen on sex. *(Long pause.)*
CROYDON. Who was the lady?
NATTRESS *(going out)*. No idea . . .
CROYDON *(running on the spot sprint)*. **Run it cold!** *(As he runs, FINNEY comes in, with a newspaper under his arm. He watches CROYDON for a moment. CROYDON finishes, heads for the door to the shower.)* Hello, son. Didn't know you were a member.
FINNEY. Don't go out. *(CROYDON disappears.)* **Don't go out!** *(Long pause. FINNEY doesn't move. Sounds of showering off. At last NATTRESS appears, towelling his head.)* My baby's dead. *(NATTRESS stops towelling.)* What do you say? *(Pause.)* My baby's dead.
NATTRESS *(deeply puzzled, begins to dry his hair)*. I'm not sure I —
FINNEY. **Don't dry your head!**
NATTRESS *(complying)*. I thought . . . excuse me, but I thought you were the Beast of God —
FINNEY. My **new** baby! *(Pause.)*
NATTRESS. Well, which one is —
FINNEY. Don't laugh.
NATTRESS. I am not laughing.
FINNEY. **You burned her in the fire! Don't laugh!**
NATTRESS. Look, I am not laughing —
FINNEY. **I am not mad.**
NATTRESS. All right.
FINNEY. I am **angry** but not **mad**!
NATTRESS. All right.

FINNEY.   You burned the warehouse and she was in there! *(NATTRESS walks a little way away.)* You burned it and my wife was there!

NATTRESS.   **Wife** now?

FINNEY.   Look, you burned the warehouse.

NATTRESS.   Did I . . .

FINNEY.   **I am not mad!** *(CROYDON appears. NATTRESS shakes his head at him to urge him to keep silent.)*

NATTRESS.   Trying to help.

FINNEY.   It's in the paper. It's her necklace. It is her! **Look at the paper!** *(He thrusts it at* NATTRESS *.)*

CROYDON.   Don't thrust. It's rude. *(NATTRESS takes the paper, looks at it.)*

NATTRESS.   I am very sorry that someone has died. Nobody should have been in there. People shouldn't be in places that do not belong to them. I think that's fundamental. It is what England used to be about. The peasant had his common and the lord the manor. That seems very reasonable. People must know what is theirs or else you get this kind of thing, you get this loss of life which I deplore.

FINNEY.   Listen — you are not listening to me —

NATTRESS.   I am. I am saying what a good example of the breakdown of our values this tragedy illustrates.

FINNEY.   **She was pregnant and she's dead!** *(Pause.)*

CROYDON.   I am going to sound thick now. I am going to sound thick as shit or thicker. But I thought you did your family in. *(Pause.)* In which case I am at my wit's end to discover —

FINNEY.   We have to keep our country decent. We can't have murder going on. I thought there might be times when you could do it but it isn't **right.** *(He looks at them.)* Is it? *(Pause.)* We must be **right.** *(Pause.)* I have got to tell the police.

CROYDON.   Loony. *(NATTRESS tries to warn him off by shaking his head, but in vain.)* What you have just said you loony is inconsistent. You are **loony.** *(NATTRESS gestures him to get away. Reluctantly he withdraws across the gym. Pause.)*

NATTRESS.   I like you, Finney. *(Pause.)* No, terrible start. *(Pause.)* I mean I care for you. Do you know why? *(FINNEY shakes his head.)* I care for you because I think you are the stock of England. In my black moments I used to wonder if people like you still existed. I thought they were all killed in the war or had gone to Australia. But then I find one, and I know the spirit lives. Is thriving. And I have to stand back and admire it, because I am in the presence of a sort of purity. *(Impatiently,* CROYDON *comes forward to interrupt, but stops on receipt of a killing look.)* If there is one thing I hate it is sounding phoney. But there are times you have to run the risks of taking yourself seriously. I love my country. Do you believe me? *(FINNEY nods.)* I love the place. It might amuse you, but I have kissed it. I have lain on my back on a clifftop, with the sun in my eyes and the gulls screaming and I have had to turn right over and kiss it, the grass, the chalk or whatever. I have done that. Have you? *(FINNEY shakes his head.)* Just an example. Nothing special. And when my country needs me, I have to respond to it. I was a major in the war. A volunteer. I was in the shambles down in Greece. Nothing heroic, but

I did it for my country, simply for my country, and I think you would have done the same. I am blind to everything except that one thing and when I think of it, I find I'm not alone. I see a line of ghosts behind me reaching two abreast, beyond Dunkirk, the Somme, the Crimea. I am in the company of decent Englishmen, and if I shudder sometimes at what I may be called upon to do, I still do it, for those ghosts, you see? *(Long pause.)*

FINNEY.   I'm sorry. I think we must be decent. First and foremost. Even before the ghosts. And you have killed somebody.

NATTRESS.   You have to go steady with decency. It is inflammable, you see. You have to know when to use it and —

FINNEY.   I don't see there is anything else, is there?   *(Long pause. CROYDON comes over.)*

CROYDON.   You want to fetch a policeman?

FINNEY.   I'm sorry but I do. *(Pause. NATTRESS drifts out, sadly.)*

CROYDON.   We'll fetch you one.

FINNEY.   No, it's all right, I can —

CROYDON.   Get you one. *(He goes out. The door is locked behind him. When FINNEY goes to try it, it doesn't budge. He comes back slowly to the middle of the gym.)*

FINNEY.   Sir Philip Sydney was a gentleman. When he was dying after a battle he had a cup of water given him. Just as he was going to drink it he saw an ordinary soldier shouting 'water! water!' so he gave it to him. That was decent. My mother had the painting hanging on my bedroom wall. **Thy need is greater than mine.** *(Pause.)* He died. Or otherwise when he got home to England he would have given away everything, presumably . . . *(The door is unlocked, and BRILLIANT comes in.)*

BRILLIANT.   Are you Finney?

FINNEY.   You know I am.

BRILLIANT.   Never mind about all that. Just say yes.

FINNEY.   Yes.

BRILLANT.   Philip Thomas Frank Finney I arrest you on three charges of murder relating to the evening of 17th September 1980. Anything you say may be taken down and used in evidence. Would you wear these handcuffs, please?

FINNEY.   **I was mad then!**

BRILLIANT *(holding out the handcuffs).*   If you would.

FINNEY *(extending his wrists).*   You did a murder.

BRILLIANT *(clipping them).*   Did I?

FINNEY.   I was with you. In the park. We did a murder.

BRILLIANT.   Well, point that out.

FINNEY.   I will.

BRILLIANT.   In your statement.

FINNEY.   Yes, I will. **We've got to stop this killing, haven't we?**
(BRILLIANT looks at him for a moment, then leads him out. A few seconds later, CROYDON comes in with NATTRESS, both fully dressed.)

CROYDON.   I was in Malaya. Have I told you? During the Emergency. I was in the British Police. They brought me in this gook one day, this communist they would now dignify by the name of guerilla, but at the time known more rightly by the name of criminal. They brought him to me and he squatted in the corner. They used to do that, squat in the corner with hardly any clothes on, staring at you. And I said, through my boy, my Chinese boy, why do you hate the British? Standard question to which they used to spout a gobful of Mao. But he didn't. He said he hated us because he was mad, and they had told him when the British were gone, so would his madness. *(Pause.)* Fucking mad.

Blackout.

Scene Five

A beach in Devon. Sound of heavy breakers and surf. FLUX and HILARY appear in the flickering sunlight. FLUX is carrying an armful of empty wine bottles. HILARY is near the end of her pregnancy.

HILARY *(shouting).* Is it going out?

FLUX. It's on the turn, it's goin' oot!

HILARY. Give me a bottle.

FLUX *(as she takes one).* We will reach the ocean liners an' the battleships. The Russian whalers an' the Japs. In the stuffy messdecks of Liberian tankers half-breeds will squabble to read our messages. Black yankees will pore over them in the gadgety bowels of nuclear submarines.

HILARY. The first one says — *(She reads from a scrap of paper.)* MANKIND YOU ARE BEAUTIFUL. YOU SHINE WITH THE LIGHT OF DIVINITY. YOU HUM WITH THE JOY OF THE WIND. JOIN THE WORLD SPIRITUAL REGENERATION MOVEMENT, CARE OF ARCHIE FLUX, THE BEACH HOTEL, TORQUAY, ANGLETERRE.

FLUX. Cork it! *(She shoves the message in the bottle, corks it.)*

HILARY. Cork in.

FLUX. **Cast it, then!** *(With a tremendous effort, HILARY pitches the bottle into the waves.)*

HILARY. **Yip-ee!**

FLUX *(wandering towards the sea).* Look at the sea! **It's risin' up, look at the sea!**

To yells of euphoria, crashing of waves, sudden blackout.

Scene Six

The garden at Broadmoor on a summer's day. A WARDER stands near a group of men who hoe the ground. They work slowly over the stage.

WARDER *(in a mood of permanent wonder).* The person dies. The person is cremated. The person's bits go up the chimney. The person's bits fall down. The bits are swept up. The sweepings are put on the dustcart. The dustcart empties on the fields. The fields grow cabbages. The cabbages are cut down. A person eats the cabbages. The cabbages turn into bits of person. The person dies. *(Pause.)* The person is cremated. The person's bits go up the chimney. The person's bits fall down. The bits are swept up. The sweepings are put on the dustcart. The dustcart empties on the fields. The fields grow cabbages. The cabbages are cut down. A person eats the cabbages. The cabbages turn into bits of person . . . *(Pause.)* The person dies . . . *(Pause.)* The person is cremated. The person's bits go up the chimney. The person's bits fall — *(FINNEY flings his hoe down with an angry gesture, looks up into the sky. The rest hoe on.)* Dropped your hoe, Finney. *(Pause. He doesn't move.)* Finney. Your hoe. *(Pause.)* Hoe. *(Pause.)* Your hoe. *(Pause.)*

FINNEY. Not mad.

WARDER. Your hoe.

FINNEY. Not mad.

WARDER. Hoe. *(Pause.)* Hoe. *(Pause.)* Hoe. *(Pause.)* Hoe. *(FINNEY bends, picks it up.)* Many thanks. *(FINNEY rejoins the hoers.)*— fall down. The person's bits are swept up. The sweepings are put on the dustcart. The dustcart empties on the fields. The fields grow cabbages. The cabbages are cut down. A person eats the cabbages. The cabbages —

Blackout.